WHISKY

& COCKTAILS

WHISKY

MICK WÜST

AN
EASY
GUIDE

& COCKTAILS

GELDING STREET PRESS

"YOU DON'T HAVE TO WEAR TWEED OR SMOKE A PIPE TO ENJOY WHISKY. IT'S FOR EVERYONE."

A Gelding Street Press book
An imprint of Rockpool Publishing
PO Box 252
Summer Hill
NSW 2130 Australia

www.geldingstreetpress.com
Follow us! @ geldingstreet_press

ISBN: 9781922662286

Published in 2026 by Gelding Street Press

Illustrated by Ellie Grant
Design and typesetting by Sara Lindberg, Rockpool Publishing
Edited by Heather Millar

A NOTE ABOUT THE MEASUREMENTS

Please note that the cup and spoon measures in these recipes are based on Australian sizes.

1 teaspoon = 5 ml
1 tablespoon = 20 ml/⅔ fl oz
1 cup = 250 ml/8⅓ fl oz

A catalogue record for this book is available from the National Library of Australia

Printed and bound in China
10 9 8 7 6 5 4 3 2 1

FOR EVERYONE WHO HEARD
I WAS WRITING A BOOK ABOUT
WHISKY AND SAID, "LET ME
KNOW IF YOU NEED HELP
WITH ANY TASTING . . ."

NOW'S YOUR CHANCE.

COME DRINK WHISKY WITH ME.

CONTENTS

INTRODUCTION

Water of life.

Liquid gold.

Bottled sunshine.

Whisky. It's just a drink. But it's a drink that warms your chest and warms your heart. Even the word is delicious – a tender kiss, softer than fudge.

What is whisky?

Do you want the facts – or the philosophy?

On the surface, whisky seems simple enough. It's just grain, water, and yeast. Distilled beer, aged in wooden barrels.

But go a little deeper, and it's so much more than that.

It's liquid history. The drink in your glass was distilled years, or even decades ago. When you taste it, you're tasting a moment in time – like seeing the light from a star that burned out last millennium.

It's a dance of four elements – grain and peat from the earth, malted and mashed with water, distilled by fire, and aged by exposure to the air.

Whisky is a product of simpler times. It's slow and inefficient in the best way – something to hang onto in a world that's gotten too fast.

Whisky inspires songs and stirs up obsession. It's not simple at all. It's one of the most complex drinks around.

TO "E", OR NOT TO "E"?

Whisky or whiskey? What's the difference?

The rule of thumb is that Scotland, Canada and Japan (and most other countries) spell it "whisky", while Ireland and America spell it "whiskey". An easy way to remember – America and Ireland both contain an "e" themselves.

Throughout this book, I'll say "whisky" unless I'm specifically talking about American or Irish whiskey.

No one's born liking whisky. (Well, except perhaps the Scottish.)

My introduction to the glorious spirit was pre-mix cans of Johnnie Walker Red and cola. I thought I was so distinguished when I upgraded to buying Black Label to mix with Pepsi. Move over, James Bond – you're not the only one with a signature drink.

For my 21st birthday, my friends bought me a bottle of Glenmorangie Nectar d'Or. I didn't know much, but I knew you do *not* mix nice single malts with Pepsi. I endured every drop of that delightful whisky without any mixer. What a brave soul.

When my 25th birthday rolled around, those same friends chipped in and bought me a Glenfarclas 25. (Seriously, how good are my friends??) By that point, I'd actually started to appreciate neat whisky, and I sipped that stewed fruit and spice very slowly indeed.

The following year, I was nursing a glass of Caol Ila at a jazz club in Rome. The air was thick with sultry saxophone and swirling smoke, my chest was warm with smoldering peat, and I had one of those moments of unadulterated bliss: "This is the life."

I started drinking whisky in my teens because I liked the idea of being a whisky drinker. It wasn't that I wanted to look cool and impress people (well, maybe I wanted that a tiny bit). But in my mind, a whisky drinker has a kind of self-assurance. They know who they are, and they know what they like.

I've since learned that your identity doesn't come from your drink choice. But I know there are others who think whisky is for certain kinds of people, too. To some, whisky is for the cool and confident, or for society's elite. To others, it's the drink of jaded criminals and alcoholic private detectives.

Maybe the most tragic idea is that whisky is somehow a "man's drink." Not that there's anything wrong with an old white man wearing tweed and drinking single malt in a leather armchair . . . but you don't have to be one to enjoy whisky. You don't even have to own a chair.

Whisky doesn't need you to be a certain kind of person. You can wear tweed if you want, but you can also wear ripped jeans and drink highballs in the sunshine, or wear a maxi dress and sink a whisky sour, or drink old fashioneds with facial piercings.

I firmly believe there's a whisky drink to suit any person and any situation. Queen Victoria mixed whisky with red wine. Mark Twain enjoyed a hot toddy. Katharine Hepburn and Humphrey Bogart drank scotch with soda water, and Frank Sinatra was partial to a rusty nail cocktail. You think whisky should never be mixed? Take it up with Little Vic and Ol' Blue Eyes.

A lot of myths have grown up around whisky, mostly among those who *do* want to look cool and impress people.

Ever heard that the older the whisky, the better it is? Take that with a grain of salt – older is *different*, but not always better.

Ever heard that scotch is superior to bourbon, or that single malts are better than blended whiskies? These just aren't true – different whisky styles are simply *different*.

And despite what some Very Serious People say, there's no right way or wrong way to drink whisky. You can drink it neat, on the rocks, mixed with cola, or in a cocktail. (I've even heard of people using single malt in jelly shots. I'm not sure what to do with that information.) The golden rule is: preference, preference, preference. As long as you're enjoying what you're drinking, you're doing it right.

If I could go back in time, I'd tell my younger self he can mix that Glenmorangie with Pepsi if he wants. It's there to be enjoyed, not placed on a pedestal.

"Come guess me this riddle:

What beats pipe and fiddle?

What's hotter than mustard and milder than cream?

What best wets your whistle?

What's clearer than crystal?

Sweeter than honey and stronger than steam?"

"The Humours of Whiskey" (Irish folk song)

Whisky is incredibly complex. I've written books about beer and gin, but this is the book that tied me up in knots again and again. There is so much about the way whisky's made, the way it tastes, the culture that's risen up around it, the different approaches in different countries . . . it can get ridiculously confusing, and make you feel kind of stupid.

But that's exactly why I distilled all of that into one small book. To make the confusing stuff a bit clearer. To help you feel a bit smarter. To give you enough information to understand and appreciate whisky . . . without getting too caught up in all the technical mumbo jumbo.

No assumptions.

No jargon.

No rules. (Except this one – don't order "two fingers of whisky" unless you're in the City of Angels in the 1930s and some dame just broke your heart.)

Just enough knowledge to help you explore, enough ideas to inspire you to try new things, and enough factoids to impress (and sometimes irritate) your friends.

I don't know if this book will change your life . . . but I'm confident it will change the way you drink whisky.

Expect to mix a few concoctions that would make whisky snobs gasp.

Expect to get some stains on this book.

Expect to have a helluva lot of fun.

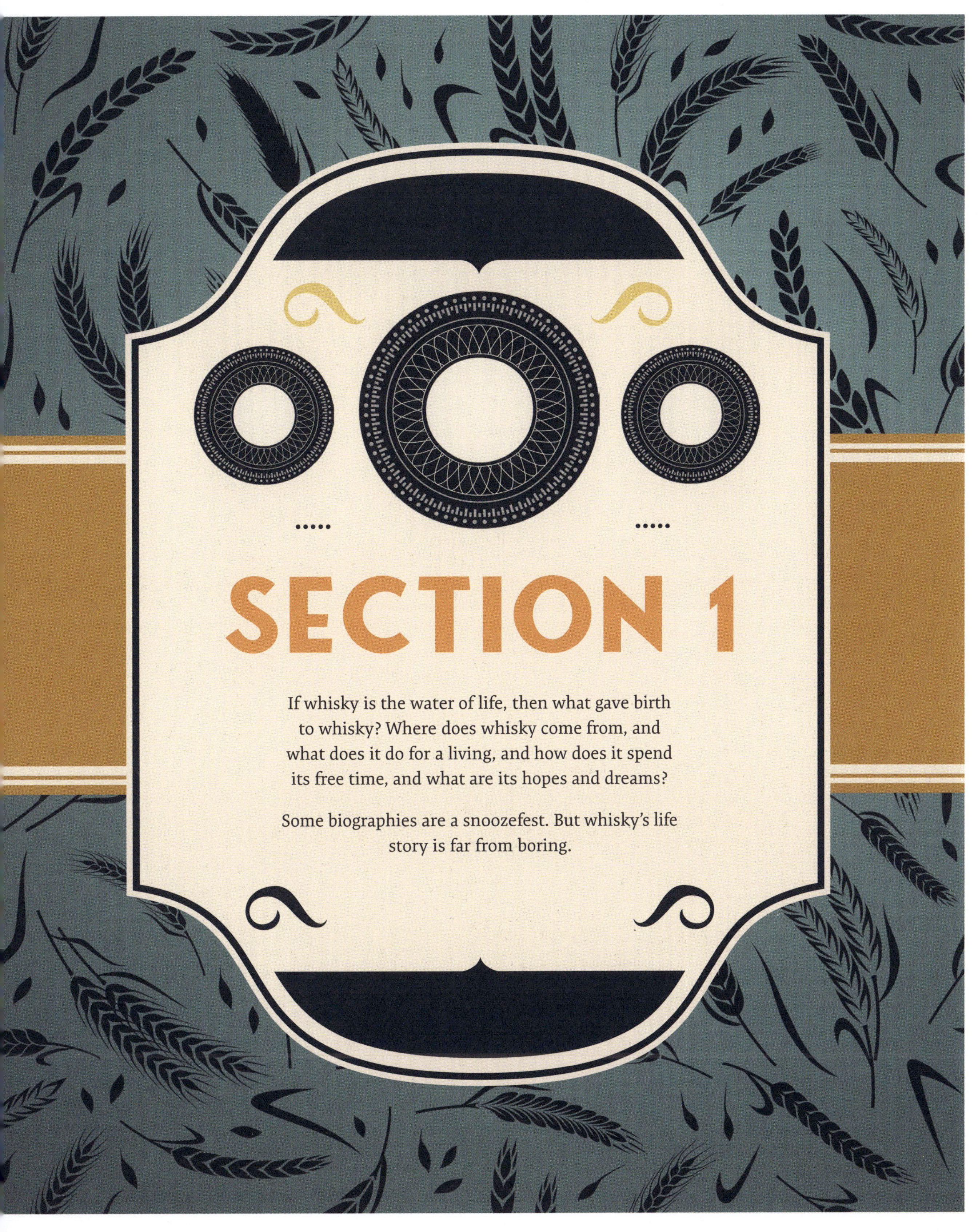

SECTION 1

If whisky is the water of life, then what gave birth to whisky? Where does whisky come from, and what does it do for a living, and how does it spend its free time, and what are its hopes and dreams?

Some biographies are a snoozefest. But whisky's life story is far from boring.

HISTORY ACCORDING TO WHISKY

The people who invented distilling thousands of years ago weren't trying to make booze; they were making perfume and medicine. And the ancient alchemists who first turned wine into spirits were trying to make gold or the elixir of life. (Their discovery eventually led to whisky, so I say they succeeded!)

Both the Scottish and the Irish claim they were the first to make the drink we call whisky, and I'm not getting in the middle of that fight. I've seen *Braveheart*.

Either way, it was about 1000 years ago. Farmers had excess barley that would spoil if it just sat around in their barn in the damp. And monks who'd returned home from a missionary trip in Europe had learned the skill of distillation. The monks' recipe and the farmers' barley made whisky, which lasts longer than barley – if you don't drink it first.

Back then, most whisky was drunk straight off the still – a raw, clear spirit with nasty flavors you'd cover up with spices and honey. Eventually, people discovered that storing this spirit in wooden barrels turns the rough spirit into smooth, richly colored whisky. You might even say it turns to gold.

When whisky started to spread across the globe, each place had their own take on it. In Scotland and Ireland, they'd used barley. In North America, they used mainly rye and corn and developed their own distinct styles of whisky.

And when whisky headed to Japan, rather than evolving over centuries at the hands of farmers and monks, it hit the ground running in the hands of artisans, scientists, and corporations.

Let's take a ride through some of the milestones in whisky's history. It's complex, and we're going to be jumping between countries a lot. If you feel yourself getting travel sick . . . well, apparently whisky's medicinal.

Circa 1200 BC – An Akkadian tablet describes a primitive form of distillation being used in Mesopotamia . . . to make perfume, not boozy drinks. Boring.

Circa 100 AD – In Egypt, an alchemist called Mary the Jewess is (probably) the inventor of the three-armed *tribikos* – the great grandma of the modern pot still.

Circa 800 – Arabic alchemist Jabir ibn Hayyan develops the alembic pot still in his quest to turn metals into gold. The gold thing doesn't happen, but he discovers how to distill wine into spirits. Win some, lose some.

Circa 1000 – Scottish and Irish missionary monks bring home a souvenir from their trips to Europe – the secret of distillation. Spirits are mainly used for medicine; it'll be another few centuries before people are drinking them for fun.

Circa 1300 – People are calling distilled spirits *aqua vitae* – "water of life." Arnaldus de Villa Nova says, "It prolongs life, clears away ill-humours, revives the heart, and maintains youth." Aqua vitae is translated *uisce beatha* in Ireland and *uisge beatha* in Scotland – the origins of the word "whisk(e)y."

1324 – In Ireland, a religious manuscript called the Red Book of Ossory contains the earliest recorded recipe for distilling aqua vitae. Instead of distilling with wine, they use local barley. We can start calling it whiskey now, but it's spiced and unaged; it'll be a while before it looks like the drink we have today.

1405 – An Irish chieftain dies in 1405 after drinking too much of the stuff at Christmas – "not aqua vitae to him, but *aqua mortis*."

1495 – In Scotland, King James IV sends malt to a friar with the royal order to make 1500 bottles of whisky. He most likely wanted it for making gunpowder, trying to turn metal to gold, or creating the elixir of life. And you thought the most badass thing you could do with whisky was drink it.

1505 – The Guild of Barber Surgeons are granted exclusive license to produce whisky in Edinburgh. These guys started as barbers for the monks, used their razors to perform surgeries, took up distilling alcohol for medicinal use, then got a monopoly on whisky. Talk about a career move.

1536–1541 – King Henry VIII dissolves all the monasteries in England, Wales, and Ireland. How will all those monks make a living? By making spirits. As their secrets spread, people start distilling in homes and on farms.

1556 – In Ireland, the (English) Parliament declares whiskey, "a drink nothing profitable to be drunken daily and used, is now universally throughout this realm made," and makes it illegal for common people to distill without a license. Irish distillers happily ignore this law.

1608 – King James I grants a license to Sir Thomas Philips to distill whiskey on his land. Bushmills claims this date as their origin (it's on every bottle), though the Old Bushmills Distillery wasn't founded there 'til 1784. Either way, Bushmills is the oldest licensed whiskey distillery in the world.

1644 – In Scotland, Parliament introduces an excise tax on spirits . . . which causes illicit distilling to skyrocket. Over the next 200 years, a series of taxes and bans on whisky are all unsuccessful. Scots will dodge taxes, start riots, and run illegal distilleries. What they won't do is stop drinking whisky.

1700s – Scottish and Irish immigrants flock to America, bringing their fiery passion for making whiskey – and the name "whiskey" itself. They quickly adapt to using the locally grown rye, and whiskey spreads through the Colonies.

1780 – In Dublin, a Scottish lawyer named John Jameson starts a distillery. Today, Jameson Irish Whiskey is still the most popular Irish whiskey.

1783 – In the area that will become Kentucky, distiller Evan Williams opens the first commercial distillery of the United States. Unlike the northerners using rye, he's blissfully making whiskey out of local corn. This is the beginning of bourbon, even if it's not called that for another 60 years.

1785 – In Ireland, the authorities introduce a tax on malt. It's meant to raise funds and hurt bootleggers. Instead, crafty distillers replace a portion of their malted barley with unmalted barley, giving rise to a distinctly Irish style – pot still whiskey.

1791–94 – In America, Alexander Hamilton imposes the infamous Whiskey Tax, sparking the Whiskey Rebellion. The new nation barely avoids civil war when 7000 rebels march on Pittsburgh, and George Washington conscripts 13,000 troops to disperse them. (Why wasn't any of this in the musical?!)

1801 – Up in Canada, the first major whisky producer is John Molson, who starts a whisky distillery with a copper pot still that was used for rum. He'll also become the first exporter of Canadian whisky, sending his booze to England when the Napoleonic Wars cut off their French brandy supply.

1802 – Back in the States, recently elected President Jefferson repeals the Whiskey Tax. He also incentivizes farmers to move to the Kentucky area and grow corn. What do farmers do with an abundance of corn? Make whiskey.

1820 – In Scotland, a 14-year-old boy opens a grocery store in Kilmarnock. He sells malt whisky made by local distillers and will eventually start blending whiskies together and selling the blends under his own name. His name? John Walker – but you can call him Johnnie.

1822 – In Australia, a 26-year ban on distilling is lifted. The colony's first (legal) whisky distillery opens in Tasmania – the Sorell Distillery – and over a dozen more follow. But in 1838, the governor outlaws distilling in Tasmania after his wife says, "I would prefer barley to be fed to pigs than it be used to turn men into swine." Luckily, her words and his law don't affect mainland Australia. Oink oink.

1823 – Scottish Parliament passes a new Excise Act, making it easier and more profitable for illegal distillers to go legit. The following year, George Smith gets a license for his previously illicit distillery. Other distillers eventually follow suit, moonshining drops off, and the modern era of scotch whisky distilling begins.

Oh, and Smith's distillery? Glenlivet, which today is the oldest legal distillery in Scotland.

1830s – In Tennessee and Kentucky, many distillers are using the sour mash method – adding grain from previous runs of whiskey to new batches. Scottish chemist James Crow uses new technology and techniques from Scotland – and science! – to perfect the method.

1831 – In Ireland, Aeneas Coffey patents his version of a column still, which allows for continuous distilling. This faster and cheaper way to make smooth, consistent whisky is a game changer – it takes off in America and leads to the invention of blended scotch. But in Ireland, the big distilleries reject column stills.

1850s – In Tennessee, an enslaved man and skilled distiller named Nathan "Nearest" Green teaches a boy named Jack Daniel how to make whiskey, including his method of filtering it with sugar maple charcoal to mellow it out. Green will later become the first master distiller for Jack Daniel's distillery – hired as a free man – and his method of filtration is a key characteristic of Tennessee whiskey.

1852 – Charles Dickens exchanges whisky by post with Irish writer Robert Bell, receiving "two bottles of genuine Irish" and sending a "specimen" of Glenlivet scotch. (I had to include something about writers enjoying whisky, didn't I?)

1860–1880s – An aphid-like insect wipes out over half the vineyards in Europe. The resulting shortage of French brandy in Britain has many turning to Irish whiskey or the new blended scotch, which is now seen as a refined drink. Spirits dealers start exporting scotch to the USA and around the British Empire. By the early 20th century, Scotland will overtake Ireland as the world's largest whisky producer.

1890 – Canada sets the first-ever regulation around the minimum age of whisky – Canadian whisky is required to be aged for two years.

1915 – In the UK, the Immature Spirits (Restriction) Act says whisky must be aged for a minimum of three years. It's meant to hurt the whisky industry, which has recently been rife with inferior unaged spirits. Instead, the Act raises whisky back to premium status and cements the practice of barrel aging.

1918 – A Japanese sake brewer named Masataka Taketsuru arrives in Scotland. He studies chemistry and learns the traditional art of Scottish whisky making at several distilleries. Five years later, Shinjiro Torii – founder of drinks giant Suntory – will employ Taketsuru to open Japan's first whisky distillery, Yamazaki.

1920–1933 – Prohibition in the USA. The only whisky people are drinking is homemade, bootlegged, or legal "medicinal" whisky. (Pharmacies become *very* popular.) Since America is a major market, Prohibition forces many distilleries around the world to close. Canadian and scotch whisky will bounce back after Prohibition ends; for Irish whiskey, the hard times will continue . . .

1922 – Ireland gains independence from Britain, leading to Irish distillers losing their largest export market – the British Empire.

1933 – Scotch is defined in UK law for the first time.

1934 – In Japan, Taketsuru leaves Yamazaki to open his own distillery. His company will become Nikka – a great rival of Suntory.

1960s – In Australia, a change in the way spirits are taxed sends the remaining whisky industry into a tailspin, causing it to crash in the 1980s – with no survivors.

1963 – At a time when blended scotch is all the rage, Glenfiddich introduces single malt as a premium style in the USA. This marketing move will begin single malt's (eventual) rise to a place of prestige.

1964 – The US Congress declares bourbon whiskey a "distinctive product of the United States" (in the way that scotch is distinctive to Scotland). Bourbon will build a name for itself around the world.

1980s – Whisky falls out of vogue and the world enters an economic recession, leaving Scotland with warehouses full of whisky that no one wants to buy. This surplus, known as the "Whisky Loch," leads to the closure of many distilleries – some temporarily, some forever.

1988 – The release of "Classic Malts of Scotland," a collection of six single malts from different scotch regions, brings single malts into the spotlight. The world is beginning to appreciate whisky again.

1989 – In Australia, Bill Lark starts the fight to make smaller-scale whisky distilling legal again (it was outlawed in 1901) – and wins. In 1992, he'll open the first distillery in Tasmania in 150 years – Lark Distillery – and resurrect the Aussie whisky industry.

1993 – The father of the American craft beer movement, Fritz Maytag, starts Anchor Distilling. In an effort to emulate America's earliest whiskeys, he revives pot distilling and makes Old Potrero, a 100% rye whiskey.

2001 – Japanese whisky grabs the attention of the world when Nikka's 10-year-old Yoichi Single Malt wins *Whisky Magazine*'s "Best of the Best." It's the first time a non-Scottish whisky has won.

2009 – The Scotch Whisky Regulations 2009 define five legally protected scotch regions: Highland, Lowland, Speyside, Campbeltown, and Islay.

2010 – Dalmore releases Trinitas 64 Year Old, a whisky that contains vintages from 1868, 1878, 1926, and 1939. It's the first whisky to sell for over £100,000 per bottle. It won't be the last.

2014 – Australia's Sullivans Cove wins "World's Best Single Malt" at the World Whiskies Awards. Then Taiwan takes the podium in 2015 (Kavalan); Ireland in 2019 (Teeling); England in 2022 (The Lakes) and 2024 (The English), and Israel in 2023 (Milk & Honey). World-class whisky is made all around the world.

2017 – In honor of Nathan "Nearest" Green, entrepreneur Fawn Weaver founds Uncle Nearest, which will become the most successful Black-owned distillery in the world. Its award-winning master blender, Victoria Eady Butler, is Green's great-great-granddaughter and the first Black female master blender.

2021 – Demand for Japanese whisky around the world is massive, but lack of regulation means that not all whisky in Japan is actually Japanese, or truly whisky. New labeling standards are finally put in place to legitimize Japan's excellent contributions to the global whisky scene.

2022 – In Scotland, a trustee at Blair Castle finds a hidden cellar door while cleaning. Inside are 40 bottles of whisky casked in 1833 – the oldest whisky in the world. The trustee doesn't hesitate to take a bottle home and drink it. Perk of the job.

2025 – Booze writer Mick Wüst still hesitates to drink his bottle of 25-year-old Glenfarclas.

203
523
87

WHISKY TODAY

Imagine if you had to visit an Irish monastery or a Scottish farm every time you wanted a whisky. Don't get me wrong – it'd be worth the trip. But thankfully, nowadays it's a bit easier to get your fix.

Pretty much anywhere in the world, you can walk into a bar and take your pick of whiskies from distilleries across the globe.

Huge distilleries and tiny distilleries; ones making traditional styles, and ones experimenting with new methods; distilleries older than your grandaddy, and distilleries so new you haven't heard of them. You can drink a whisky that tastes like it did a hundred years ago, or one that's been infused with peanut butter.

And it's not just the liquid that's spread around the world – it's the entire culture that's built up around it.

Try explaining whisky blogs and YouTube reviews to those Irish monks.

Try telling those Scottish moonshiners hiding in the hills that distillers would receive global awards and spruik their wares at international whisky festivals.

Or convincing the pioneers distilling corn in Kentucky that diehards would bid thousands of dollars at auctions to buy rare bourbons.

Even a few decades ago, no one would have believed that average punters would buy whisky subscriptions and invest in whisky barrels, or that millions of tourists would visit distilleries to see how the golden liquid is made.

Whisky's bigger than the Beatles – and it's still growing.

WHISKY BOOM

It's easy to forget how much Prohibition shattered the whisky industry. The Great Depression and a couple of world wars didn't help. Thousands of distilleries across North America closed, the Scottish and Irish whisky industries shrank to a handful of large companies . . . even 50 years after Prohibition ended, the whisky industry was a shadow of its former self.

But now, new whisky distilleries are popping up like malty mushrooms. How did we get from there to here?

We all needed to learn a few lessons.

Bigger isn't always better

Through the 20th century, the global whisky industry survived because of big corporations with deep pockets. The little guys wouldn't have made it on their own.

But with the big boys running the show, things were done their way. Make whisky in huge production facilities. Choose grains and yeast and methods that yield the highest volume of whisky, rather than the most flavorsome. Make the easiest-drinking whisky to reach the broadest market of drinkers.

It's a good way to maximize profits and please your shareholders. It's also a good way to turn the world of whisky into a homogenous blur – a packet of brown crayons.

To get the spectrum of colors, you need the variety that small distilleries bring.

In the 1990s, a scattering of brave visionaries started to challenge the status quo in the whisky world. Inspired by the early craft beer movement, a few small distilleries opened up and started making whisky.

They could only make a fraction as much whisky as the big distilleries, and they couldn't compete on price. But their passion and their stories were unique, and their whiskies were unlike anything else available.

Stop playing it safe

In the 1960s and '70s, heaps of people were drinking whisky, but most of it was from a few popular brands that aimed to be as accessible as possible. No one wanted distinctive spirits or acquired tastes. They wanted easy drinks – wham, bam, thank you dram.

Then whisky fell out of fashion, replaced by even easier drinking spirits like vodka and white rum, usually hidden in sugary cocktails.

Whisky couldn't compete with vodka when it comes to minimal flavor. It was time to go in the other direction by returning to an old style of whisky – single malt scotch.

Single malts don't blend in. With their quirky, regional, sometimes intense flavors, each one doesn't have the mass appeal of an easy-drinking blended whisky. But lots of distilleries making different whiskies means a whole big box of colorful crayons to choose from.

Glenfiddich and a few other distilleries had started bringing their single malts to the rest of the world, but in the late 1980s the big corporations really got behind them and gave them a push.

Single malts were a wake-up call: "You don't have to play it safe." And as drinkers became interested in the distinct personalities of each region, each distillery, each whisky, this magic spread wider.

With drinkers ready to explore, distillers *everywhere* could explore. Some recaptured historic styles, while others experimented with new ones. Some used traditional ingredients and methods, while others innovated.

There's still plenty of money to be made in high volumes of whisky with low flavor – it's the business model for some of those large companies.

But now it's also profitable to make whiskies that put flavor first.

Great whisky can come from anywhere

While the rise of single malts did boost the profile of flavorsome whisky across the board, it was still scotch getting all the highest praise on the world stage.

If you found yourself among whisky connoisseurs in the 1990s, you could safely declare, "Bourbon's for cowboys, Irish whiskey's for Irish coffee, and Canadian whisky is only good in ginger ale. Scottish whisky is the original and the best!"

Then in 2001, there was a watershed moment: a Japanese whisky won *Whisky Magazine*'s "Best of the Best" award beating out all the Scottish whiskies. Around the world, most whisky lovers had never considered Japan was making top tier whisky. This award had them rushing to try it for themselves.

It also acted as a catalyst for drinkers to seek out whisky from *other* countries. It was like something had clicked in their minds: "Great whisky can come from anywhere. I need to find it."

There's more than one way to drink whisky

People who enjoy drinking whisky are eerily good at scaring people away from whisky.

They give newcomers the impression that whisky is only for men, or only for people who know a lot about it, or only for drinking in cool weather (none of which is true).Some whisky lovers tell newcomers they must drink whisky neat (also not true).

And so people get the impression whisky isn't the drink for them, and go off to find something sweet, or something cold, or something that doesn't have so many rules.

Thankfully, whisky people are becoming more inviting: distillers are getting better at showing how versatile whisky is, offering up creative pairings and serving suggestions; bartenders are introducing people to classic whisky cocktails, and developing interesting new recipes all the time; non-judgmental whisky writers are recommending mixing different whiskies with cola or coconut water or green tea (cheers Dave Broom).

We haven't finished learning this lesson yet. But whisky is slowly shaking off the rules.

BIG WHISKY VS SMALL WHISKY

The number of whisky distilleries has shot up in the last couple of decades, with explosive growth around the world.

The new distilleries are mainly small ones, but the vast majority of whisky is still made in big distilleries. A handful of conglomerates are making more whisky – and more money – than all the rest combined.

Big Whisky

Whisky's a big drink. And whisky's big business.

It's sobering when you learn how many whisky brands are owned by the same corporations. Most of Scotland's distilleries are owned by a few companies; two dueling giants dominate the Japanese whisky industry; in America, over 90% of whisky produced comes out of a small number of very large distilleries.

English dynamo Diageo – or should I say, its global collection of distilleries – is the world leader in whisky production, but the runners up ain't too far behind. French company

Pernod Ricard rules supreme in Ireland and comes second in Scotland, and Japan's Suntory has a firm foothold in every major whisky region. The next 10 or so companies in line are hardly tiny, either, even if they're only worth a few measly billion dollars.

You'll occasionally hear people talk about Big Whisky as though it's an evil entity. They'll tell stories of larger companies muscling smaller whisky brands out of the market, of bean counters telling their own distillers to cut corners to save a few bucks . . . and unfortunately, some of these stories are true. Hurray, late capitalism.

But that doesn't mean they're supervillains. For the most part, these organizations are full of incredibly skilled people who are passionate about whisky. They're not just pumping out one spirit and slapping 50 different labels on it.

These multinational groups are to thank for so many excellent whisky brands being available all around the world. Big Whisky has kept many historic distilleries open, and revived others that would otherwise have remained closed. If it weren't for the corporates buying up brands, there'd be a lot more abandoned distillery buildings full of spiderwebs and bats.

Bigger isn't always better . . . but it isn't always worse, either.

Small Whisky

It's true that most whisky on the market comes out of big distilleries. But for every elephant, there are hundreds of monkeys dancing and swinging in the trees (or so Disney films have led me to believe). In the same way, there are plenty of small distilleries making whisky around the world.

"Small distillery" is a flexible term. It can mean three people with an old pot still, or an urban distillery selling 100,000 liters of whisky each year. But it's not only a matter of size; there's something distinctive about these smaller operations, which is why we have that sexy, hard-to-define term: "craft distiller."

Everyone has their own idea of what makes a craft distiller, but it's usually some combination of factors.

They innovate and experiment. It's easier to take a risk and try something new with a few hundred liters than several thousand. Without corporate looking over their shoulders and asking "How much . . .?", craft distillers get up to all kinds of mischief, asking "What if . . .?" and "How far . . .?" They look to the past, and rediscover processes and styles of whisky the big distilleries have forgotten. They look to the future, taking whisky where it's never been before. They dabble in interesting ingredients that cost more, and processes that are less efficient. This makes for a higher price tag, but lovers of crafty whisky are happy to pay.

Their whisky varies from batch to batch. Global whisky brands ensure their flagship product or core range has a consistent taste, and their customers expect it. But small distilleries don't have master blenders with access to thousands of casks, so each batch of their whisky is unique. This isn't a shortcoming – there's beauty in the differences. Just as wine connoisseurs appreciate the differences in each vintage of wine, fans of craft whisky enjoy the distinctive personality of each batch.

They're more engaged with their customers. While huge distilleries need to appeal to a huge customer base, smaller distilleries don't need to reach everyone – they can focus on the people in their local area or tap into the corners of the internet where whisky nerds hang out. As a result, they tend to have a small but fiercely loyal following.

They follow passion over profit. Small distillers aren't just driven by the market – they make the whisky they want to make. They still need to run a sustainable business and earn a living. But if money was all they wanted, they'd be working at a bank. Instead, they're sweating next to a hot copper still for long hours to make something they hope they'll be able to sell several years from now.

It takes a lot of patience and courage to be a small distiller. (Unless your parents are rich. Then you're fine.) So visit your local distilleries, spread the word, and show your support. It makes a difference.

Sometimes it's hard to tell how big a whisky brand is. In a world where the global whisky brands use words like "traditional," "artisan" and "handmade" in their marketing, it can be hard for the little guys to stand apart.

But while it's tempting to think of small distillers and giant corporations like a David vs Goliath story, it's not always that clear cut. The big whisky companies invest heaps in research and innovation, there are family-owned businesses with huge production distilleries, and plenty of craft distilleries are actually owned by the multinationals.

I love supporting small distillers, but I'm not a placard-wielding, "Boycott the capitalist fatcats!" kind of person. Those fatcats make some damn good whisky, too.

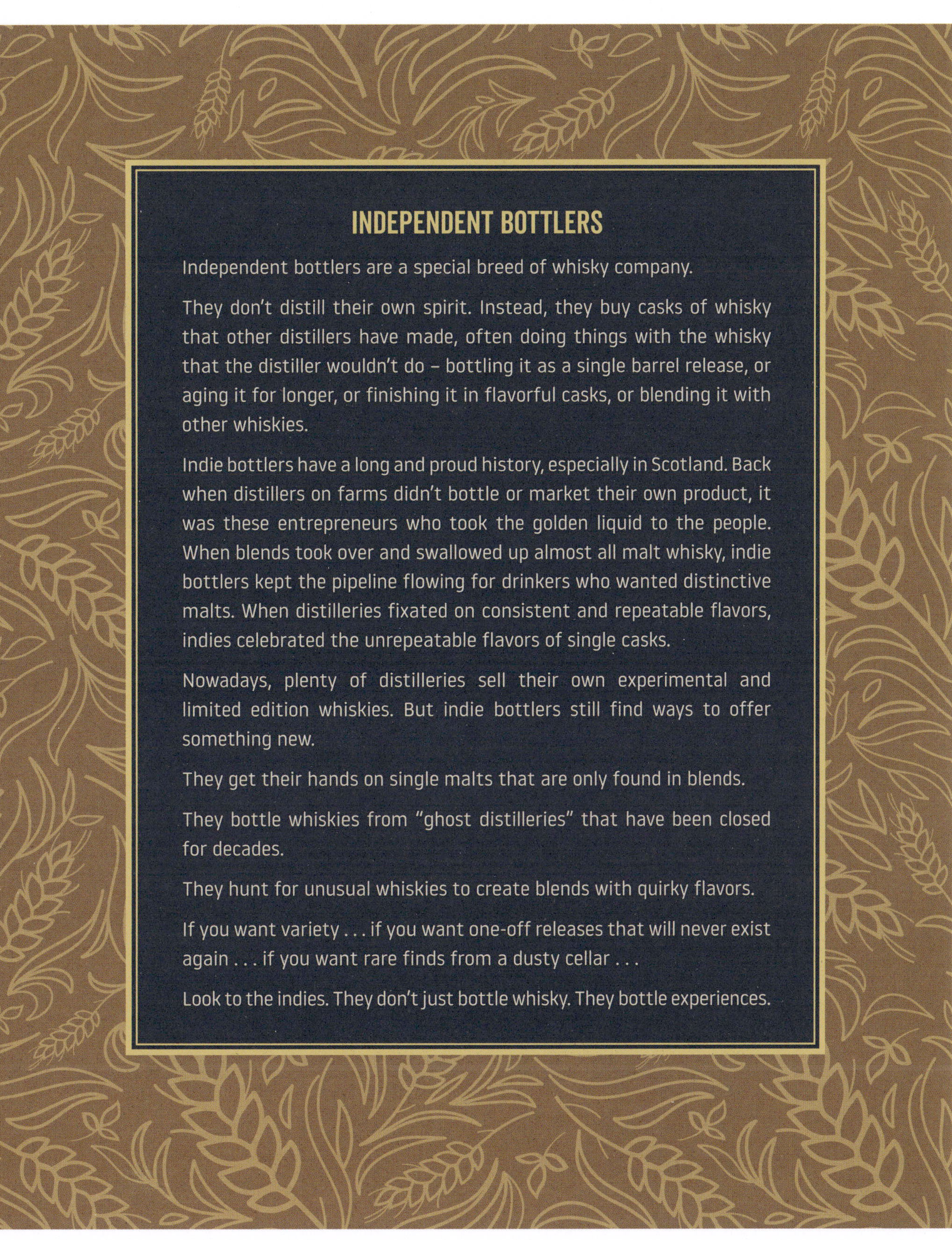

INDEPENDENT BOTTLERS

Independent bottlers are a special breed of whisky company.

They don't distill their own spirit. Instead, they buy casks of whisky that other distillers have made, often doing things with the whisky that the distiller wouldn't do – bottling it as a single barrel release, or aging it for longer, or finishing it in flavorful casks, or blending it with other whiskies.

Indie bottlers have a long and proud history, especially in Scotland. Back when distillers on farms didn't bottle or market their own product, it was these entrepreneurs who took the golden liquid to the people. When blends took over and swallowed up almost all malt whisky, indie bottlers kept the pipeline flowing for drinkers who wanted distinctive malts. When distilleries fixated on consistent and repeatable flavors, indies celebrated the unrepeatable flavors of single casks.

Nowadays, plenty of distilleries sell their own experimental and limited edition whiskies. But indie bottlers still find ways to offer something new.

They get their hands on single malts that are only found in blends.

They bottle whiskies from "ghost distilleries" that have been closed for decades.

They hunt for unusual whiskies to create blends with quirky flavors.

If you want variety . . . if you want one-off releases that will never exist again . . . if you want rare finds from a dusty cellar . . .

Look to the indies. They don't just bottle whisky. They bottle experiences.

HIBIKI
SUNTORY WHISKY
JAPANESE HARMONY
A meticulous blend of the finest selection of whiskies

WHISKY AROUND THE WORLD

Those Irish monks and Scottish farmers would be amazed to see how far whisky has traveled . . .

In England, they've always enjoyed a simple scotch and soda, but one fancy cocktail bar makes a bacon and egg martini – a whiskey sour made with bacon-infused Jack Daniels, garnished with a rasher of bacon and a Haribo fried egg lolly.

In France, where they drink more whisky per capita than any other country, you can find French whiskies made with spelt or buckwheat, aged in wine barrels or fruit brandy casks.

In Switzerland, head into the alps and visit Devil's Place bar in St Moritz, which holds a world record for having over 2500 different whiskies from 20 countries. What better way to warm up after a ski?

In Canada, you can drink whisky in a tunnel stocked with over 300 unique whiskies – an homage to the secret passage built by the founder of Canadian Club, whose own tunnel went from the distillery in Ontario to his house in Detroit.

In Japan, whisky highballs are everywhere. You can get one expertly crafted by an artisan bartender who hand-carves the ice . . . or poured from a highball machine that chills and carbonates with high-tech precision . . . or in a can from a vending machine.

In India, enjoy fine aged international whiskies in a luxurious bar furnished with Chesterfield sofas and rare antique books. Or walk through the visitor center of a single malt distillery and learn about the increasingly sophisticated art of Indian-made whisky.

In Hong Kong, you can sip blended scotch and green tea as a cocktail in a classy hotel bar . . . or as a sweet mixed drink in a karaoke room, poured from plastic jugs for a hit of caffeine and liquid courage.

In Australia, you can hit up the greenest distillery in the world, powered by used cooking oil from the roadhouse next door, with the whisky malted in an old (sorry, "reclaimed") tumble dryer. Or head to an inner-city bar for a frozen whisky cocktail from a slushie machine.

In New Zealand, you can't go past The New Zealand Whisky Collection cellar door in Oamaru. Drink whisky made in the 1990s in a building built in the 1880s, then walk down the road to see a colony of the smallest penguins in the world. (Just for something different.)

From Singapore, which houses the world's largest collection of vintage whiskies in its Grande Whisky Museum, to Föhr, a tiny island off the coast of Germany where the locals are obsessed with Manhattans and tourists buy them as a souvenir . . .

. . . the whole world has gone wild for whisky.

yeast

INGREDIENTS

To make any spirit, you distill an alcoholic liquid into something stronger. But what ingredients go into that booze juice in the first place?

For whisky, you need: water, for the liquid; grain, for the sugars that will become alcohol; and yeast, for turning those sugars into alcohol.

Well, that's what *goes into* making the spirit. But for whisky, there's also what the spirit *goes into*: wooden casks. Whisky wouldn't be whisky without these.

WATER

Any distiller will tell you: to make good whisky, you need good water – and lots of it.

In ye olde days, distillers had to set up shop next to a reliable water source; you won't find any old distilleries in the middle of a desert. The quality of their water would affect the quality of their whisky. Full of cholera and dead frogs? Not ideal. And while distillers of the past didn't always know this, the mineral levels in each particular water source can impact the yeast during fermentation, which affects the final flavor of the whisky.

Nowadays, many distilleries still sing the praises of their water source: it bubbles up from an ancient underground spring, or it's been filtered through volcanic rock, or it trickles down from melting mountain snow. They'll say it's the reason their whisky can never be imitated.

It makes for great storytelling. But the full truth is slightly less romantic: in the modern world, plenty of distilleries around the world use tap water. It's clean, it's convenient, it's consistent, and it's been quality-tested. And if it's not exactly the way they'd like it to be, that's okay – we live in the future! Technology is magic! Distillers can add or remove any minerals they want. They analyze and alter their water chemistry like wizards making potions. A distiller can make their water profile mimic the Kentucky River, or a Scottish loch, or a Japanese volcanic spring.

Water's a vital ingredient in whisky, and I hope distilleries keep talking about their mystical springs and picturesque rivers. As long as they know a distiller on the other side of the globe can imitate that unique water with Google and a chemistry set.

GRAIN

Every spirit begins with a source of sugar. Brandy gets its sugar from grapes, rum gets its sugar from sugarcane, and whisky gets its sugar from grain.

While the sugars in grapes and sugarcane are ready to go, the sugars in grain are complex and unfermentable; the tiny yeast can't work with them. They need to be broken down into simple sugars that the yeast can eat, like when you cut up food into small pieces for a toddler.

There's one ingredient that is particularly skilled at breaking down these sugars. So before we look at the other kinds of grains that can go into whisky . . .

Let's talk about malt.

What's malt?

Depending on the context, "malt" can refer to malted barley (an ingredient) or malt whisky (a style of whisky made with malted barley). Plenty of scope for confusion. Here, we're talking about the ingredient.

Malt is the result of a process called malting, which helps raw grain to unlock those unfermentable sugars. Once upon a time, distillers would malt their own grain, but nowadays most buy it in from commercial maltsters.

Malting begins with soaking the raw grain kernels in water, which tricks them into thinking they're about to grow into a plant. The grains respond by breaking down the complex sugars they've been holding onto, ready to use them as energy to help them grow big and strong. But before they can use their sugars for growing, the maltster stops the process by drying them out with hot air or smoke.

What once was raw grain now has a new destiny – instead of becoming a barley plant, it will become whisky.

Barley isn't the only grain that can be malted, but it's the most common by far. When it comes to unlocking the sugars for fermentation, barley has the most keys. It's not just that barley is excellent at breaking down its *own* complex sugars, but it has a superpower where it can also help unlock the sugars in *other* grains during the mashing stage. It's a superhero acting for the good of all grainkind, and it's in almost every whisky you'll ever drink.

Kinds of grain

BARLEY

In Scotland and Ireland, barley's always at the center of the conversation. Even in the USA and Canada, where corn and rye are the superstars, malted barley is usually there as an indispensable ally.

It's easy to think early Scottish and Irish distillers must have used barley because it had the best flavor, but really, they used what was readily available: farmers grew barley for food, and the excess became booze.

Nowadays, many distillers still choose barley because it's better than other grains at producing alcohol, so it simply makes more whisky.

Most distillers use pale **malted barley – AKA malt –** which tastes nutty with a gentle sweetness. Its flavors can be subtle in whisky, but most malt distilleries are relying on other elements to contribute the majority of the flavors. To them, the malted barley's main job is to produce maximum alcohol.

Some new craft distillers add **specialty malts** into the mix. These yield less alcohol than standard distiller's malt but also develop more complex flavors – think biscuit, toast, caramel, toffee, chocolate, and coffee notes.

Unmalted barley is found in the unique Irish style called pot still whiskey. There it brings nutty, fruity and spicy notes, and an almost creamy texture.

Peated malt is a whole 'nother beast. (See "Peat" on page 43.)

CORN

Corn is rich with complex sugars and has a fancy schmancy name to fall back on – "maize" – but it's the salt of the earth.

Corn's willing to get messy. It doesn't complain when it's cooked into an unappealing slurry. It doesn't even complain when malted barley swoops in at the last minute and gets the credit for making those sugars fermentable.

Corn makes up the majority of bourbon, Canadian whisky, and some other grain whiskies, and provides the lion's share of booze. Despite this, it rarely gets the chance to stand in the spotlight, since its critics say corn spirit is "one-dimensional" (rude). Corn generally shares the stage with other grains, and they get the praise for the flavor. Never mind that corn's adding to the mouthfeel, and helping to accentuate those sweet vanilla, honey, and caramel notes.

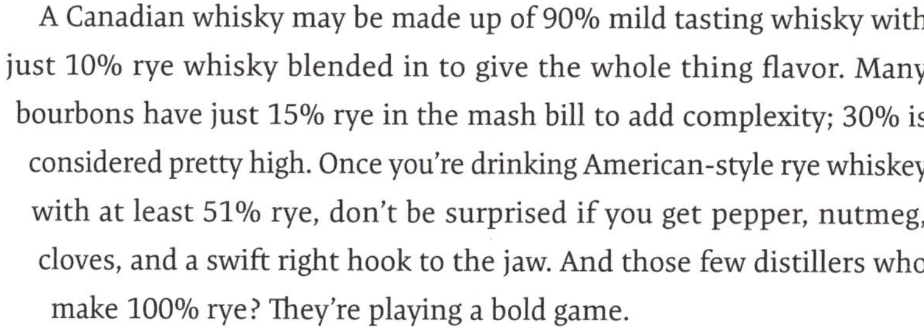

It ain't glamorous. It's hard work. But someone's gotta do it – and corn's happy to step up.

RYE

You know that friend you have who's "not for everyone"? They're sarcastic and cynical. Some people find them abrasive and offensive. Others think they're the most interesting person in the room.

Rye is that friend.

It's dry, spicy, acidic, and bitey, and its intense personality makes it perfect for balancing out a more placid whisky.

A Canadian whisky may be made up of 90% mild tasting whisky with just 10% rye whisky blended in to give the whole thing flavor. Many bourbons have just 15% rye in the mash bill to add complexity; 30% is considered pretty high. Once you're drinking American-style rye whiskey with at least 51% rye, don't be surprised if you get pepper, nutmeg, cloves, and a swift right hook to the jaw. And those few distillers who make 100% rye? They're playing a bold game.

Not everyone likes rye, but that's okay – rye doesn't need everyone to like it.

WHEAT

Wheat is the quiet friend who doesn't go to every party, and when it does show up, it usually hangs out in the kitchen and helps to clean up. Wherever wheat pops up, it makes things go smoothly.

In Scotland, grain whisky made from wheat makes up the bulk of the volume in blended scotch and lets a small amount of malt whisky bring the flavor.

When wheat's used in a bourbon instead of rye, it makes for a more mellow spirit, stepping out of the way so the flavors of the corn and barley and barrel can really shine. A portion used in a rye whiskey will let rye be rye . . . while softening the edges a little. Even in wheat whiskey, where it makes up the majority share, this grain invites the other aspects of the spirit to lead the way.

People tend to overlook wheat, but it doesn't mind. It's comfortable in its own skin. (Or husk, I guess?)

ALTERNATIVE GRAINS

Barley, corn, rye and wheat are the "big four" when it comes to whisky, but there are a number of distillers exploring other grains.

Americans are at the forefront of this, with pioneers playing around with the likes of oat, spelt, millet and triticale, and various colors of corn. (It comes in red, white, and blue – how could they resist?)

You can also try a rice whisky from Japan, a French whisky made from buckwheat (technically a pseudo-grain, but I won't tell if you won't), or an Australian whisky made from native weeping grass.

Are they "traditional" or "common" or "financially viable"? Maybe not. But why should that stop distillers – or drinkers – from exploring?

YEAST

Yeast are all around you, in the air, and on everything we touch. They're single-celled fungi, barely larger than bacteria – tiny, almost insignificant . . . that is, until you bring them together by the billions and breed them to do your bidding. They can even help make whisky.

The little critters love to chow down on sugar, so when a distiller adds them to a big vat of sweet grain water, the yeast couldn't be happier. They gobble up the yeast and spit out the alcohol that gives us that cozy fireplace feeling in our chest when we sip our whisky.

Distillers, brewers, and bakers all use a species of yeast called *Saccharomyces cerevisiae*, but they use different strains. Just as terriers were bred to hunt rats, Dobermans to be guard dogs, and toy poodles to fit into a handbag, people have bred one species of yeast to be good at different jobs.

Many distillers use a yeast strain bred to be quick, efficient, and tough. They want a lean, mean, booze-making machine that can handle a lot of sugar, a lot of heat, and a lot of alcohol . . . so they can make a lot of whisky.

But alcohol isn't the only thing yeast can create. Scientists have isolated over 200 flavor compounds yeast can produce during fermentation – a variety of fruity, floral, and spicy flavors. That's a lot of flavor potential for whisky!

More and more distillers are now using strains of yeast that have been bred for particular aromas and flavors, even though they can be less efficient at producing alcohol. Think of them like a worker who takes a longer lunch break but uses the time to strum tunes on their guitar – they may get a bit less work done, but everyone gets to enjoy listening to their beautiful music.

Whether a distiller is going for booze or complex flavor notes, there's one thing they'll agree on: yeast plays a huge role in creating whisky.

So raise a glass to these microscopic maestros. Without them, we'd be drinking barley water.

CASKS

There's an old Scottish saying: "The wood makes the whisky."

In one sense this means "the wood is the most important factor," but the saying is almost literal, too. Because while a distiller can make those first three ingredients into spirit, it's the wood that turns that spirit into whisky.

What kind of wood?

Oak is the favorite, and has been for an awfully long time. The two most common kinds used for aging whisky are European oak and American oak.

European oak has a fairly tight woodgrain, which limits how much the spirit can soak into the wood, and how quickly it can pass in and out of the wood. So European oak has a slower, more subtle influence on whisky, but it can give notes of wood and spice.

American oak has a more open woodgrain, so has a quicker, more intense influence on whisky, and is known for giving sweet vanilla and coconut notes.

In recent decades, distillers have been having fun with casks made from other woods that lend interesting flavors to their whisky. They generally use them just to "finish" the whisky, rather than for the full maturing period.

Mizunara (Japanese oak) is inconvenient in almost every way – it's hard to acquire, it's expensive, it's crooked, it's knotty, it's prone to leaking – and yet it offers some intriguing flavors such as Japanese incense and sandalwood.

Amburana is a South American wood that serves up cinnamon, baking spice, and vanilla.

Australian red gum is a hardwood used by a few Aussie distilleries, bringing intense flavors of menthol, honey, and eucalyptus. (Perfect if you're making whisky for a koala.)

Then there's the sweet and fruity influence of **cherry wood**, the nutty and rich flavors of **chestnut**, the sticky sweetness of **maple.**

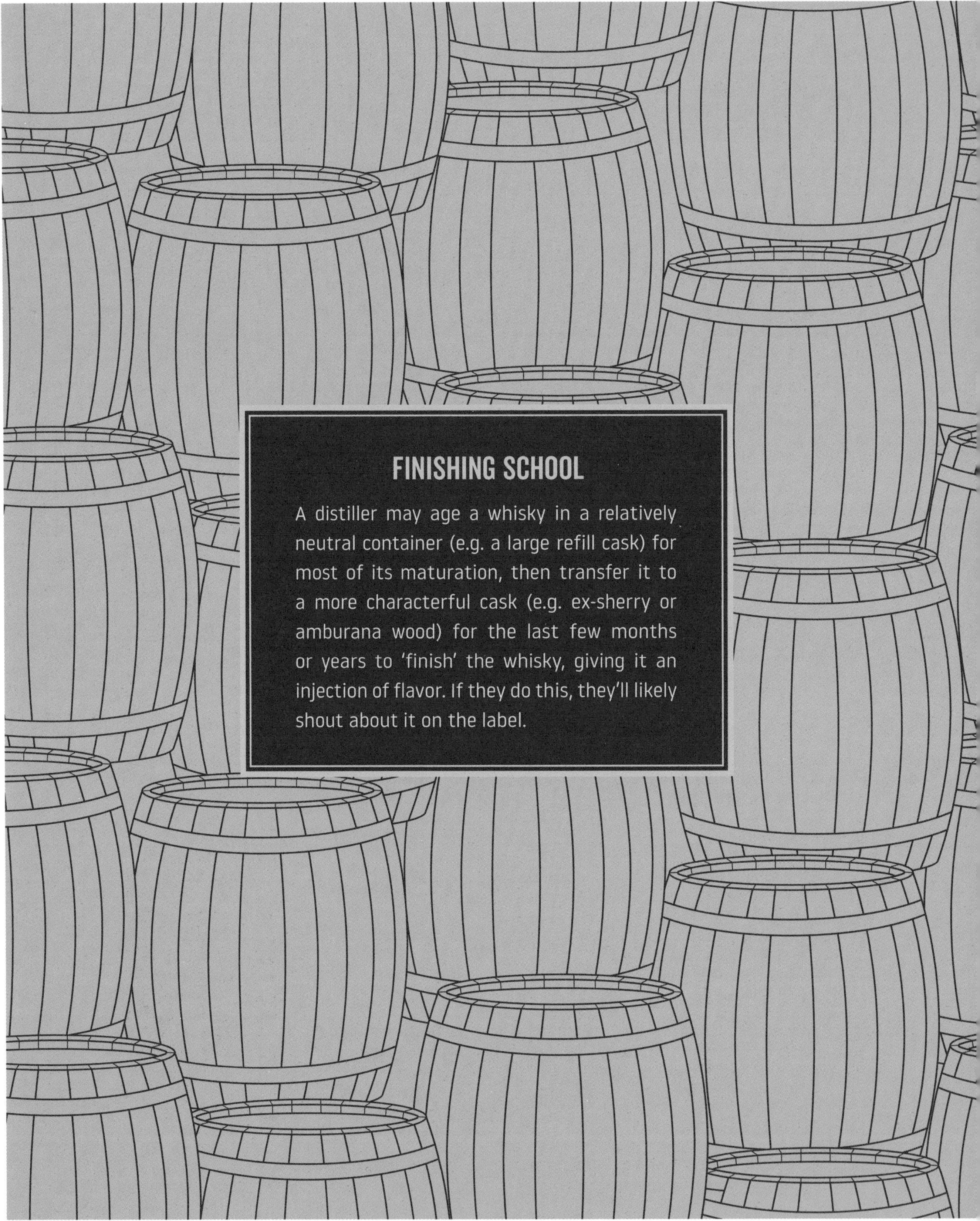

FINISHING SCHOOL

A distiller may age a whisky in a relatively neutral container (e.g. a large refill cask) for most of its maturation, then transfer it to a more characterful cask (e.g. ex-sherry or amburana wood) for the last few months or years to 'finish' the whisky, giving it an injection of flavor. If they do this, they'll likely shout about it on the label.

How much has the cask already been used?

Some whiskies are made in brand new wood, and others are aged in barrels that have been used before. Newer or "fresher" barrels can impart a lot of character in less time, while older barrels tend to work better for longer, slower maturation.

Virgin oak hasn't held any other alcohol before, so it's got plenty of character from the wood itself to give to whisky. By law, bourbon must be aged in charred virgin oak.

First fill casks are being used to age whisky for the first time since being used for another drink like port, sherry, or wine. These casks serve up maximum color and flavor from their previous tenant, since there's still liters of the stuff soaked in the wood!

Second fill casks have already been used to age whisky since holding something else, so they give less intense, more balanced character from the previous wine or spirit.

From the third fill onwards, casks are considered **refill** casks. These don't have much flavor left to give, so they allow the nuances of the spirit itself to shine more.

How big is the cask?

Smaller casks have more influence on whisky more quickly, due to their higher ratio of wood-to-whisky. (It's a surface area thing. Please don't make me do the maths.)

If a distiller wants to age a whisky for a long time, they'll want a larger cask so the wood doesn't overdo it. But if they want a shorter maturation, a smaller vessel can speed things up. Barrels come in several standard sizes, from the 120-liter quarter cask up to the 500-liter butt. (Must . . . not . . . laugh . . . at . . . butt . . .)

What was in the cask before?

If the barrel is repurposed, the wood will bear the stamp of the previous occupant: both the flavor, and also the way it interacted and the chemical components left behind.

Bourbon casks can't be re-used for bourbon, so there's an abundance of bourbon barrels available for distillers around the world to use. Since the high ABV bourbon has already sucked out most of the flavor compounds from the wood, the barrel is left as a relatively low impact vessel, giving gentle oak flavors like soft vanilla and honey. This means they're excellent for long aging, since they won't accidentally over-oak the whisky and dominate the flavor.

Casks that used to house **sherry** provide sweet fruity notes – think rich fruit cake and sticky dried fruits. Whisky labels may even mention the kind of sherry that was in the barrel, such as Oloroso or Pedro Ximénez (PX).

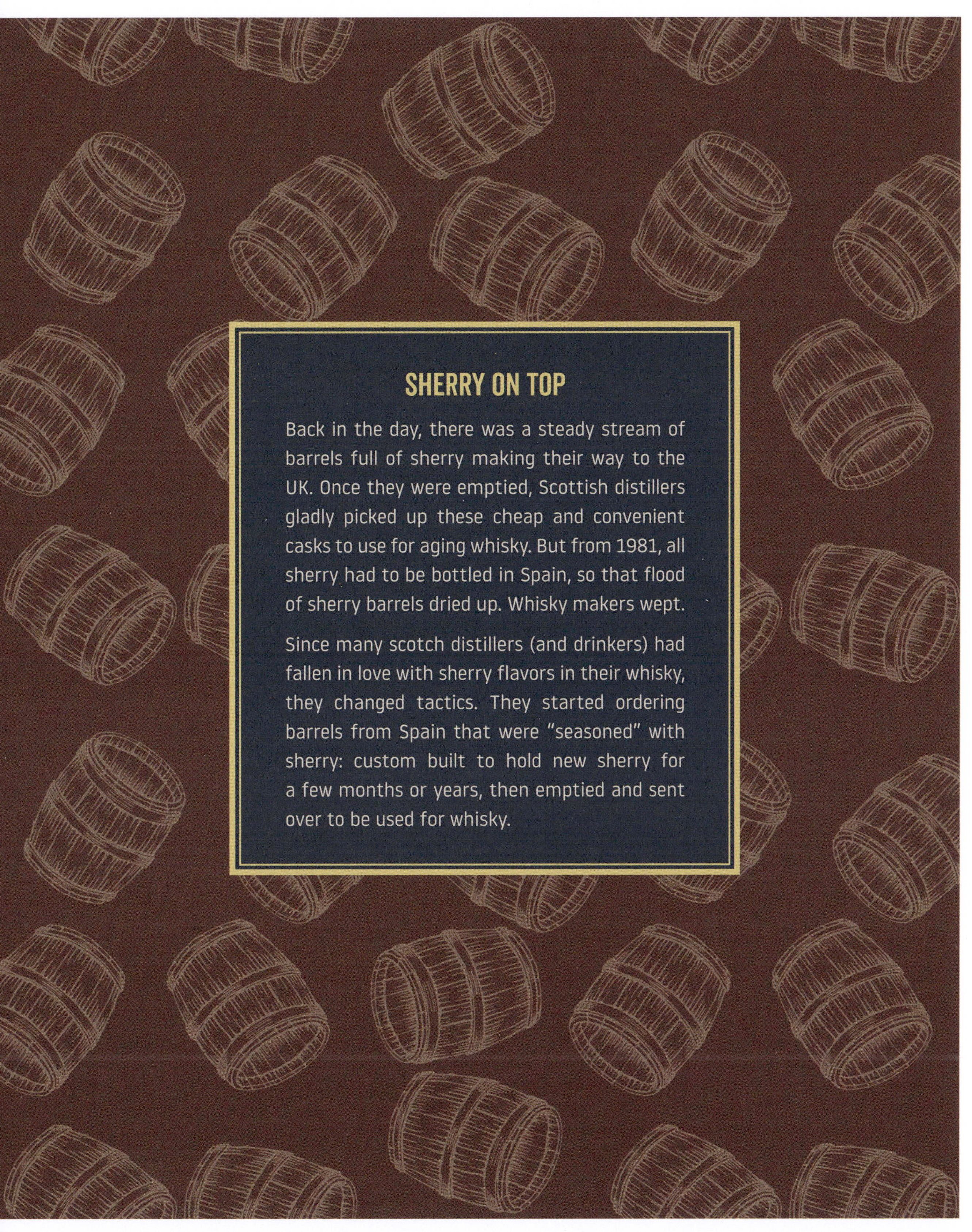

SHERRY ON TOP

Back in the day, there was a steady stream of barrels full of sherry making their way to the UK. Once they were emptied, Scottish distillers gladly picked up these cheap and convenient casks to use for aging whisky. But from 1981, all sherry had to be bottled in Spain, so that flood of sherry barrels dried up. Whisky makers wept.

Since many scotch distillers (and drinkers) had fallen in love with sherry flavors in their whisky, they changed tactics. They started ordering barrels from Spain that were "seasoned" with sherry: custom built to hold new sherry for a few months or years, then emptied and sent over to be used for whisky.

Port casks are another beloved option, since they can bring intense flavor notes of dried fruits, berries, and chocolate.

Wine barrels can bring all kinds of flavors to a whisky, depending on the wine itself.

More and more, whisky makers are playing around with all kinds of casks for maturing whisky. **Rum? Tequila? Brandy?**

Bring. It. On.

How toasted or charred is the cask?

Barrels aren't just raw wood. The oak is "seasoned" – either dried in a kiln or air-dried over many months – then the inside of every barrel is flamed. (Yes, it's as awesome as it sounds.)

Wine or sherry casks tend to be toasted just enough to activate the flavor compounds in the wood, giving gentle vanilla and nuttiness.

Bourbon casks are fired for longer and are charred until the inside is black and cracking and looks like crocodile skin. Even the layer beneath the charcoal ends up being toasted. The intense heat caramelizes the sugars in the wood, and the cracked charring lets the whisky soak deeper into the wood and draw out more flavor.

Charred casks offer up more vanilla, caramel, and toffee notes.

It may not be an ingredient in the traditional sense, but the wood really matters. You could keep all the other ingredients the same but put a whisky in a refill ex-bourbon charred American oak hogshead and it'll be an entirely different beast to one aged in a first fill toasted French oak ex-sherry butt.

(Teeheehee. Butt.)

PEAT

What's peat? It's old half-rotted plants.

Wait, that sounds disgusting. Let me try again: peat is partially decomposed vegetation from hundreds of years ago that they dig out of a bog. That's better.

Before you get too grossed out, let me assure you that peat itself is never directly added to whisky.

In a place like Scotland, where they need over a hundred words for types of rain, indoor fires are a way of life. But in parts of the country - like remote Highland areas and small islands - they haven't always had easy access to firewood or coal. So they'd dig peat out of the ground in long bricks, dry it out, and burn it.

When peat is used to dry malt, its blue-white smoke - or "peat reek" - imparts its fragrance to the malt. When that malt is used to make whisky, it infuses the spirit with smoky notes.

Peated malt isn't used in all whiskies, or even all Scottish whiskies. But when a whisky is peated, you'll know it.

The flavors of peat

Peat can bring a range of flavors to a whisky, depending on whether it's made up of woody trees, flowering heather, or seawater-soaked grasses. You could get a sprinkle of ash, a faceful of campfire, or a slap in the face with a side of bacon, or even non-smoky flavors like grassy or floral notes, deeper earthy or woody flavors, or intense medicinal or iodine flavors.

While peated whiskies have a reputation for being pungent, that's not always the case. Like anything, it can be used with subtlety and a soft touch.

Flavor compounds from peat smoke are measured in parts per million (PPM). A lightly peated whisky may contain fewer than 10PPM. A heavily peated whisky could sit up around 50PPM. In other words, a whisky with an intense peaty flavor that some people find overwhelming may only contain 50 flavor molecules from the peat smoke for every 999,950 molecules from other things. Peat is potent stuff.

It should go without saying that peat flavors are still only part of a whisky's personality, balanced out by sweet toffee or sticky dried fruit or vanilla or honeysuckle.

Though there are certainly whiskies where the peat is distinctive and dominant. A whisky that tastes like forest floor, tar, seaweed, or band-aids may not be for the faint of heart. But some people want to bathe in the stuff.

Where do the flavors come from?

Have you ever read a whisky review written by a proper whisky connoisseur? They'll speak of crisp apples and overripe plums, vanilla sponge cake and caramel sauce, red roses and cinnamon sticks and leather and tobacco and band-aids.

But distillers aren't adding these things into their whisky as ingredients. (Thank goodness! Where would they get all those band-aids from?) The vast majority of whiskies are made from just water, grain, and yeast.

So where do those flavors come from?

Some of the flavor comes from the **barrels**. But while the wood is often responsible for the *dominant* flavors, it's not where most of the *different kinds* of flavor compounds come from.

Some of it's down to the **ingredients.** Pale distiller's malt can give nutty undercurrents, while toasted or roasted specialty malts can bring notes of biscuits and toffee and chocolate and coffee. There's the peppery bite of rye and the buttery sweetness of corn. Peated malt may give a salty seaside tang, a whiff of bonfire smoke, or, yes, a medicinal band-aid taste.

A different strain of yeast can introduce different flavor compounds at the **fermentation** stage. If you taste crisp fruit like apple or pear, or tropical fruit characters like pineapple and banana, or floral notes of jasmine or geranium, you may be enjoying the offerings of those little critters.

All different parts of the **process** can influence how a whisky ends up tasting. Variations in timing and temperatures, distillation techniques, maturation and blending . . . they all contribute to the constellation of flavor. It's seriously staggering how many variables there are.

You can't always take a sip of whisky and pinpoint the source of each flavor note. Even distillers and scientists are still on a journey of discovery as they try to decipher whisky's myriad flavors.

But there's one thing you can be confident of:

No one's putting band-aids in your whisky.

MAKING WHISKY

For hundreds of years, the basics of whisky making have stayed the same. All you have to do is turn grain to malt to grist to mash to wort to wash to low wines to new make to whisky. Not confusing at all.

I'm no scientist, and I'm not a distiller – I'm a writer with a short attention span. So let's see if we can make this simple. Partly for your benefit. Mostly for mine.

A NON-DISTILLER'S GUIDE TO MAKING WHISKY

There are three stages to whisky making:

Brewing – Prepare and ferment grain sugars to get an alcoholic drink. This takes from a few days up to about a week.

Distilling – Concentrate that drink to get a stronger drink. This takes hours.

Maturing – Put that in a barrel to get whisky as we know it. This part takes a minimum of two or three years, but could be five, 10, 20, 30 . . . don't go into this line of work unless you're a very patient person.

Brewing – turning grain into beer

The distiller feeds grain to the yeast, and the yeast turns the sugars into booze. They go at it like a piranha feeding frenzy, and after two to four days they're done digesting the sugar. In its place, they've left alcohol.

Fermentation is complete, and we have beer! But it's not normal beer – it's distiller's beer, or "wash."

Distilling – turning beer into spirit

The beer already contains everything that'll end up in the spirit. But the distiller needs to separate out the stuff they *don't* want, like undesirable alcohols and sulfur compounds.

These things all evaporate at different temperatures, so distillers use this to their advantage, heating the liquid and catching the parts of the vapor they *do* want – ethanol and certain flavor compounds. It's not perfectly precise, since molecules love clinging to each other, but each distiller finds their own balance of what they catch and what they don't. It's as much art as it is science.

Eventually, we have a clear spirit that's very high in alcohol – between about 60% and 95% ABV. Some call it new make, some call it white dog, but whatever you do – don't call it whisky yet.

WHAT'S ABV? WHAT'S PROOF?

ABV refers to Alcohol By Volume. It measures the alcohol content of a liquid as a percentage.

Simple.

In the USA, many spirits have a proof measurement on the label, which is double the ABV. An 80 proof whiskey is 40% ABV, a 125 proof whiskey is 62.5% ABV . . . you get the idea.

Internationally, ABV seems to cause the least confusion.

Maturing – turning spirit into whisky

This is where a clear spirit transforms into liquid gold.

The new make spirit is a caterpillar that's ready for its metamorphosis into a boozy butterfly. So the distiller puts the spirit into its chrysalis - an oak cask - and waits. For literally years.

During that time, the spirit pushes its way into the wood as the temperature increases and retreats back into the barrel as the temperature decreases.

The cask giveth: the wood imparts sugars, tannins, and flavor compounds to the spirit.

The cask taketh: the charred wood on the inside of the barrel acts as a natural filter, stripping away undesirable compounds.

And the cask change . . . eth: small amounts of oxygen find their way into the cask, causing chemical reactions that alter the whisky.

THIRSTY ANGELS

Did you know angels drink whisky? More than that, they steal whisky.

Oak casks aren't fully airtight, so water and ethanol vapors can escape and dissipate into the air. Over the years, each cask can lose a fair amount of whisky. Scientists call this evaporation. Whisky makers call it the angels' share, and accept it as part of the process.

The distiller's most important job now? Tasting the whisky regularly and deciding when it's reached its peak.

This whisky is ready for drinking.

DIFFERENT KINDS OF STILLS

Pot stills

- Old school and low tech – like boiling a big kettle that turns beer into booze vapor.
- Produces a "less pure," lower alcohol spirit – which means more flavor compounds.
- Only does one batch of whisky at a time.
- Used for malt whisky and most small batch whiskies; half of the process for most bourbons.

Column stills

- A more complex mechanism where beer slurry goes in at the top and steam pushes up from the bottom. The steam picks up and carries the lightest compounds, taking them through the gauntlet.
- Produces a "more pure," higher alcohol spirit, with fewer flavor compounds. Can be adjusted for more or less purity.
- Runs continuously and will keep producing spirit as long as it's fed with wash.
- Used for most lighter-flavored grain whiskies; half of the process for most bourbons.

THE WHISKY-MAKING PROCESS

Large commercial distilleries may have more doohickeys and gadgets, but here's what the whisky-making process looks like on a straightforward pot still set-up.

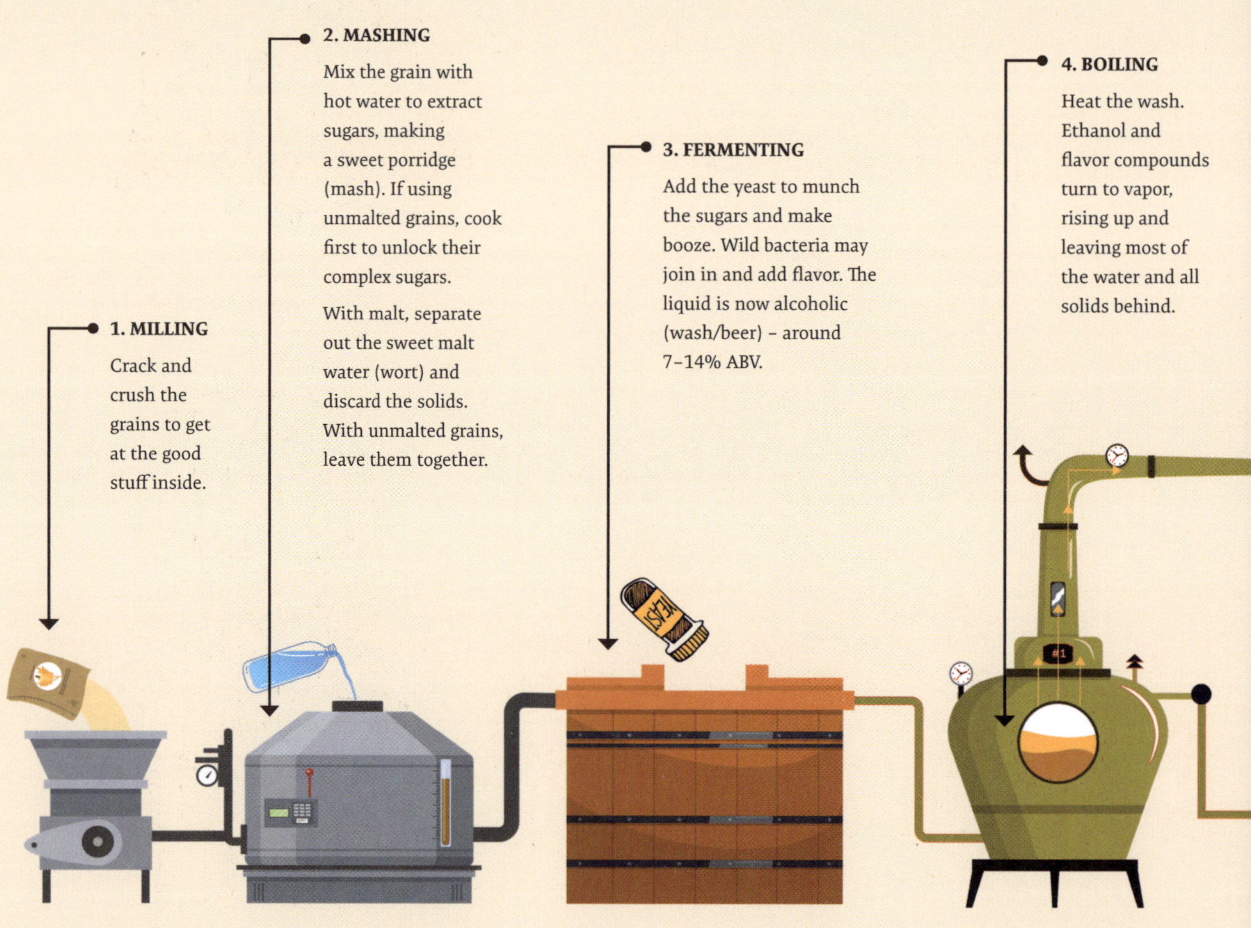

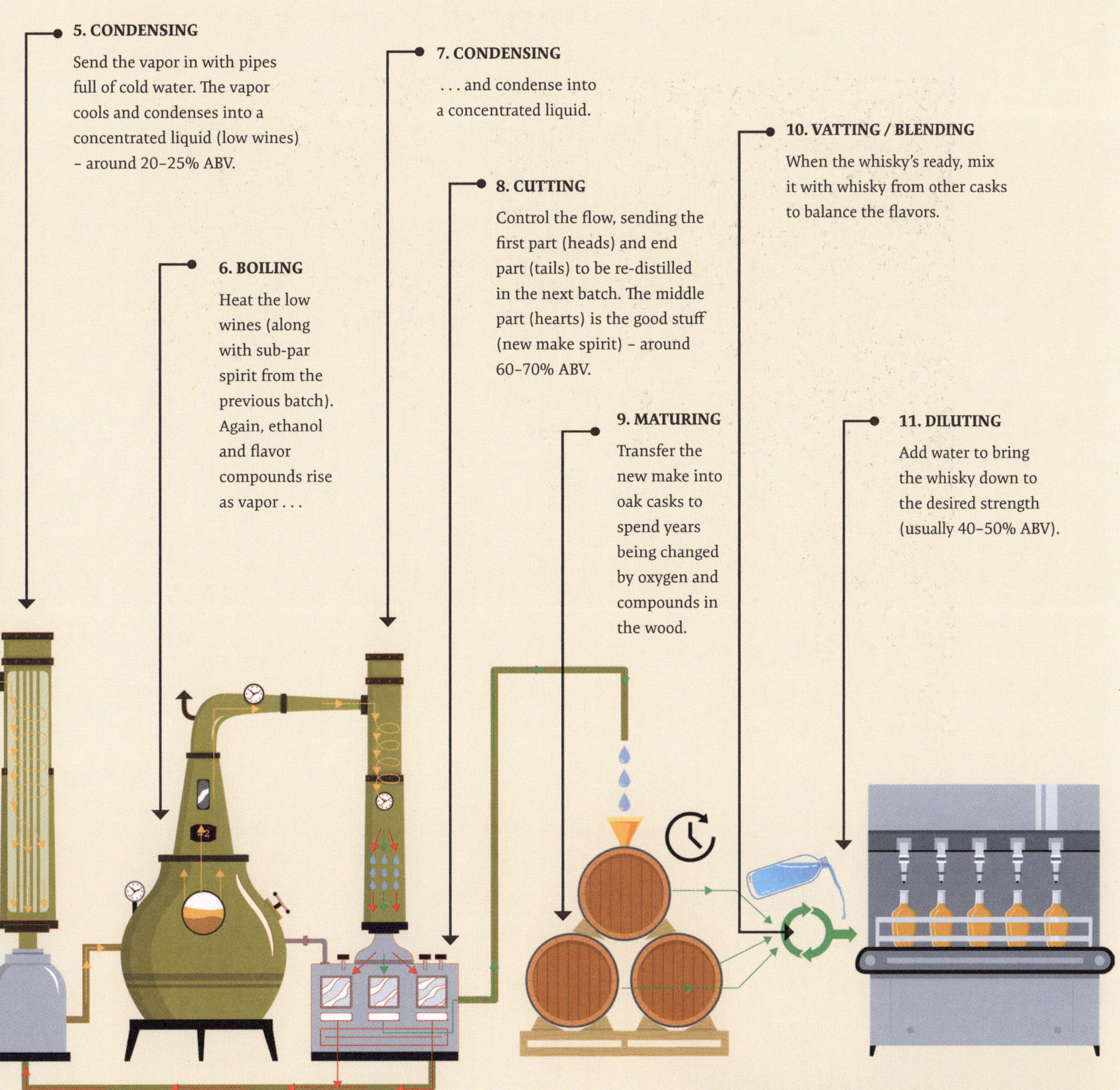

5. CONDENSING

Send the vapor in with pipes full of cold water. The vapor cools and condenses into a concentrated liquid (low wines) – around 20–25% ABV.

6. BOILING

Heat the low wines (along with sub-par spirit from the previous batch). Again, ethanol and flavor compounds rise as vapor . . .

7. CONDENSING

. . . and condense into a concentrated liquid.

8. CUTTING

Control the flow, sending the first part (heads) and end part (tails) to be re-distilled in the next batch. The middle part (hearts) is the good stuff (new make spirit) – around 60–70% ABV.

9. MATURING

Transfer the new make into oak casks to spend years being changed by oxygen and compounds in the wood.

10. VATTING / BLENDING

When the whisky's ready, mix it with whisky from other casks to balance the flavors.

11. DILUTING

Add water to bring the whisky down to the desired strength (usually 40–50% ABV).

This whisky's now ready to be bottled up, shipped out, and drunk down!

Blending

When a cask of whisky has finished maturing, it will rarely go into bottle on its own. In the vast majority of cases, distillers mix different casks and different batches of whisky together. Even single malts are made this way – though they often use the term "vatting" rather than "blending," since "blended whisky" is a different style.

But why do they do that?

Cost – releasing a barrel as a run of only a few hundred bottles is more labor intensive, more expensive to label, and harder to market and sell. This isn't viable for large distilleries working at a scale of millions of liters each year, so they mix whiskies into larger batches.

Consistency – for a brand to build a name for itself, its whiskies need to be consistent from batch to batch. No two casks of whisky ever taste the same, so the solution is to mix casks together to achieve a consistent, recognizable flavor.

Balance – a distiller may sample a cask and find that it's extracted less vanilla flavor from the oak than they wanted, or that it's had too much oxygen, or it's too acidic or too oily in the mouth, or not fruity enough. Any given cask on its own may not hit the ideal the distiller was aiming for, but mix it together with other casks and you can achieve a wonderfully balanced whisky.

Building a flavor profile – distillers are partly at the mercy of yeast and barrels when they're making whisky. They may be aiming for a specific flavor – the most subtle amount of smoke possible, or a healthy balance of toffee and apple flavors – but it's almost impossible to hit that exact target with a single cask. That's when they turn to blending, where they have much more control.

There's a reason the role of master blender in any distillery is an incredibly respected position. They're an expert with scientific precision and an artist whose creative vision reaches to the sky. These people are whisky wizards.

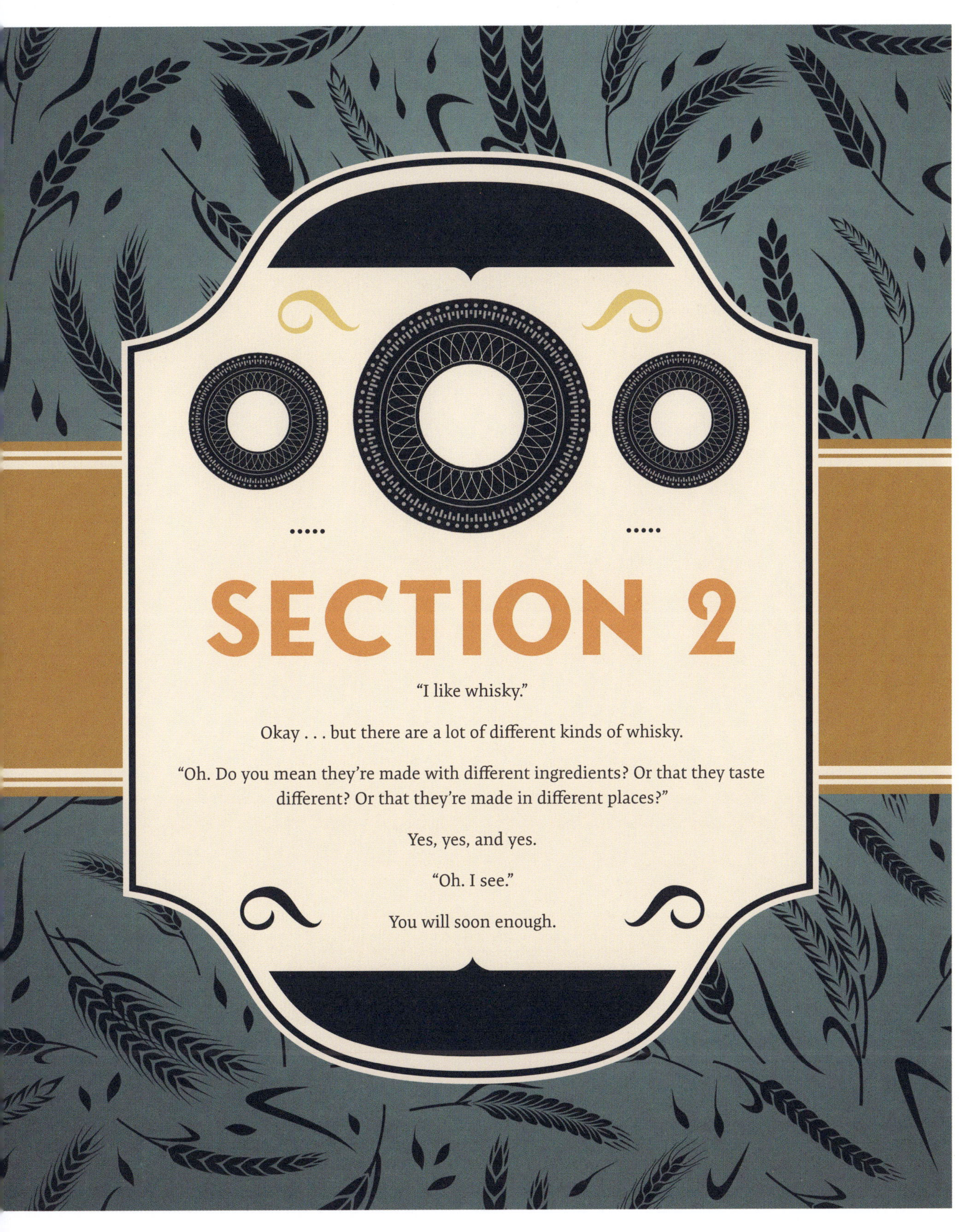

SECTION 2

"I like whisky."

Okay . . . but there are a lot of different kinds of whisky.

"Oh. Do you mean they're made with different ingredients? Or that they taste different? Or that they're made in different places?"

Yes, yes, and yes.

"Oh. I see."

You will soon enough.

Picture the scene: you're in a store, looking at shelves of whisky. You recently had a Highland single malt scotch, and absolutely adored its honeyed floral notes. So you decide to pick up another Highland single malt scotch. You take it home, pour yourself a glass . . . and it tastes *nothing at all* like the last one. It's all bacon and brine and burnt caramel.

Or perhaps you pick up a bourbon, expecting a similar experience to your last bourbon – vanilla ice cream drizzled with butterscotch sauce. But this one is spicy pepper and warm cinnamon and roasted nuts.

I love the variety available in the world of whisky . . . but it makes it bloody difficult to divide whisky into useful categories. If someone makes it sound simple, it means either:

a) they're delusional, thinking that whiskies in a particular style or region all fit into a neat little box, or

b) they're making huge generalizations, because what else can you do?

I'm definitely guilty of making generalizations all through this book . . . but I also think we can wade through the mess together.

You could spend your life arranging and re-arranging whisky into categories, the way Netflix is always trying (and failing) to sort movies into genres. Good luck trying to pin down where Pride + Prejudice + Zombies fits.

But usually, people group whisky in one of two ways: by styles or by regions.

Whisky styles are those categories like single malt, bourbon, rye, and blended whisky. This is a way of grouping whiskies based on the details of the liquid itself. What grains are in it? How's it made? What does it taste like?

Whisky regions have long been used to group whiskies based on where they come from, whether that's Scotland, America or Japan. The idea is that whiskies from a particular area often share something in common.

Which is the better way to group whiskies? Two distillers on opposite sides of the world can make whisky the same way, while two distillers down the road from each other can make totally different products. Then again, no whisky exists in a vacuum: distillers are influenced by everything from the regulations in their country, to the ingredients available in their area, to the blips of history that have changed the course of their local whisky industry.

It's all a bit of a schemozzle, really. So let's just have a crack at both.

WHISKY STYLES

To start with, let's break whisky up into three main kinds: malt, grain, and blended. Most whisky styles fit into one of these three groups. It's not always clean-cut, and the legal and technical definitions for whisky styles are different in each country . . . but most whiskies can be more or less classified this way.

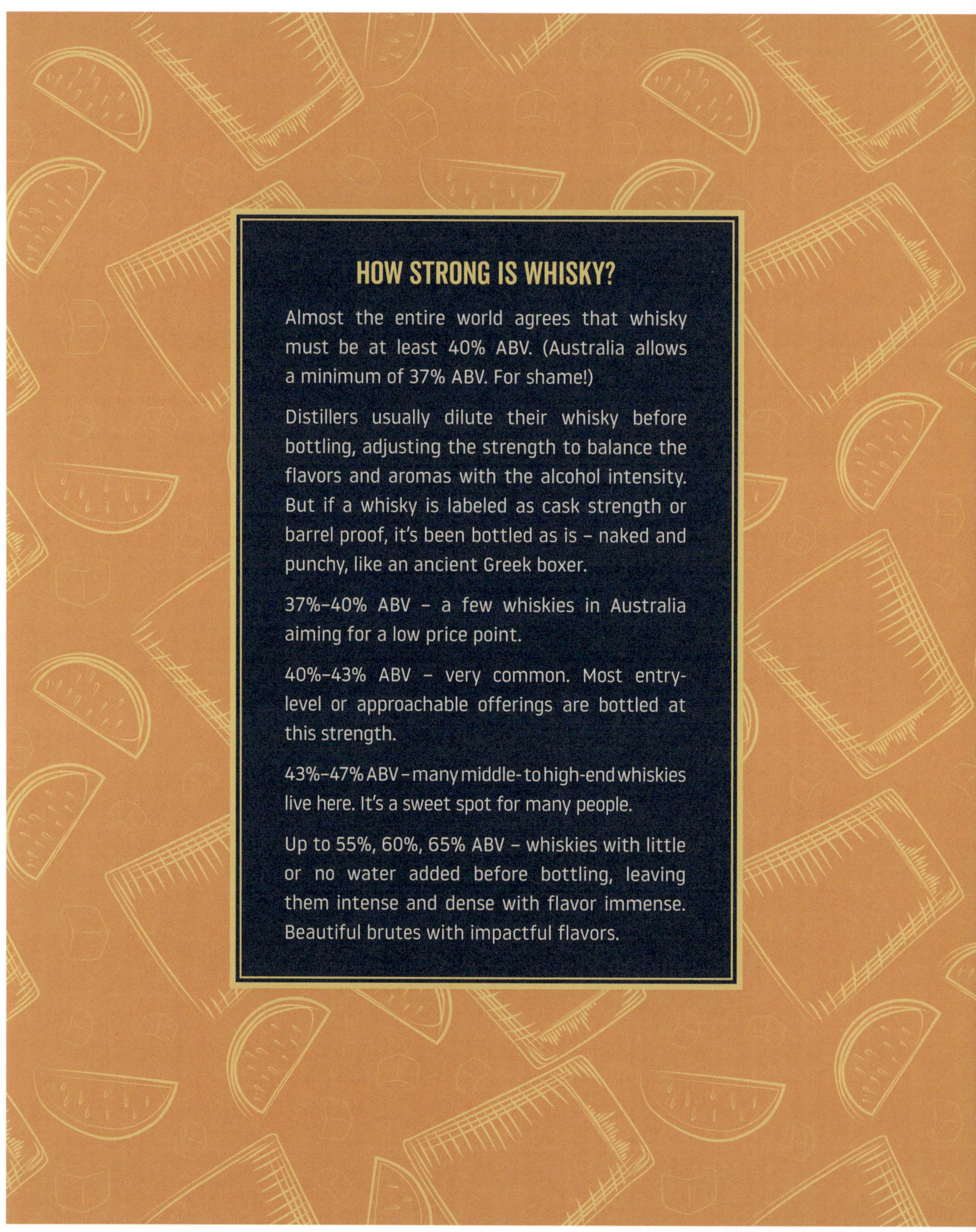

HOW STRONG IS WHISKY?

Almost the entire world agrees that whisky must be at least 40% ABV. (Australia allows a minimum of 37% ABV. For shame!)

Distillers usually dilute their whisky before bottling, adjusting the strength to balance the flavors and aromas with the alcohol intensity. But if a whisky is labeled as cask strength or barrel proof, it's been bottled as is – naked and punchy, like an ancient Greek boxer.

37%–40% ABV – a few whiskies in Australia aiming for a low price point.

40%–43% ABV – very common. Most entry-level or approachable offerings are bottled at this strength.

43%–47% ABV – many middle- to high-end whiskies live here. It's a sweet spot for many people.

Up to 55%, 60%, 65% ABV – whiskies with little or no water added before bottling, leaving them intense and dense with flavor immense. Beautiful brutes with impactful flavors.

MALT WHISKY

Malt whisky is the OG.

It's made from 100% malted barley – no unmalted barley, wheat, corn, rye, or any other grains are added. In Scotland, Ireland, and Japan, that's a legal requirement, but most distillers around the world using the term "malt whisky" are doing the same. (An exception is the "American malt whiskey" style, which only has to use a minimum of 51% malted barley. But even then, most contain more than 51% malt, and American single malts are 100% malt.)

Malt whisky is made one batch at a time in a copper pot still, which gives the spirit plenty of character – flavor compounds from the grain and from fermentation – before it even goes into barrel. (Again, legally required in Scotland and Ireland, but the done thing in most countries.)

When a single distillery makes malt whisky, it's a single malt whisky.

When malt whiskies from two or more distilleries are blended together, it's a blended malt whisky.

Single malt

Everyone's heard of single malt, whether they drink whisky or not. Just the mention of it conjures up an image of wealth and sophistication – the fancy scotch in a crystal decanter. I want to know who does single malt's PR!

But let's start by clearing up a few things.

First, throw out the idea that single malts all taste the same as each other. There's a massive range of flavor – perhaps more so than with any other kind of whisky.

Second, throw out the idea that single malts are inherently "better" than other kinds of whisky. That idea comes from a (wildly successful) marketing movement that began in the 1960s. The truth is, there are many excellent single malts, and there are many excellent whiskies that aren't single malts.

Third, throw out the idea that single malts are the most popular kind of whisky. Even Scottish single malts, which get so much spotlight, only make up just over 10% of scotch whisky.

Okay. Enough of what single malts aren't. Let's look at what they are.

WHAT MAKES A SINGLE MALT?

We've been through the basics: made with 100% malted barley; made using a copper pot still; made in one distillery. A single malt is usually made with a combination of batches of different ages and different kinds of barrels, even peated and unpeated whiskies, all mixed together. But it's all still malt whisky from the same distillery.

Scotland and Japan are famous for single malts, but most whisky-producing countries have at least some distillers who focus on them. A smart move, since single malts have a global reputation for being high quality and showcasing distinctive flavors.

So what makes single malts special? After all, blended malts are also made with 100% barley in pot stills; they're literally several single malts blended together. Is a single malt "better" than a blended malt that brings four single malts together into one bottle? Not necessarily.

The allure of a single malt is that you're not just tasting a whisky - you're tasting a distillery. Every aroma and every flavor tells the story of that distillery's DNA, its personality, what sets it apart. A distiller making single malts is like a proud parent showing you photos of their kids: "Look at my baby! Isn't she beautiful? There's no one else like her."

WHAT DOES IT TASTE LIKE?

Single malts all taste different. That's kind of the point.

Every single malt is made from 100% barley, and yet there's a remarkable diversity of flavor across the style. It's bizarre, when you think about it.

The orchestral richness of fruity and floral and spicy and smoky notes, the light or heavy body, the silky or oily or waxy texture, the sweet caress or savory bite - it all depends on how that producer makes whisky. In each sip, you're tasting the influence of that distillery's traditions, its distillers, its ingredients, its fermentation, the shape of its stills, the casks it uses, the weather patterns around its warehouse . . . every variable matters.

Read labels. Ask questions. Research the distillery. Search for reviews.

Every single malt is an opportunity to learn.

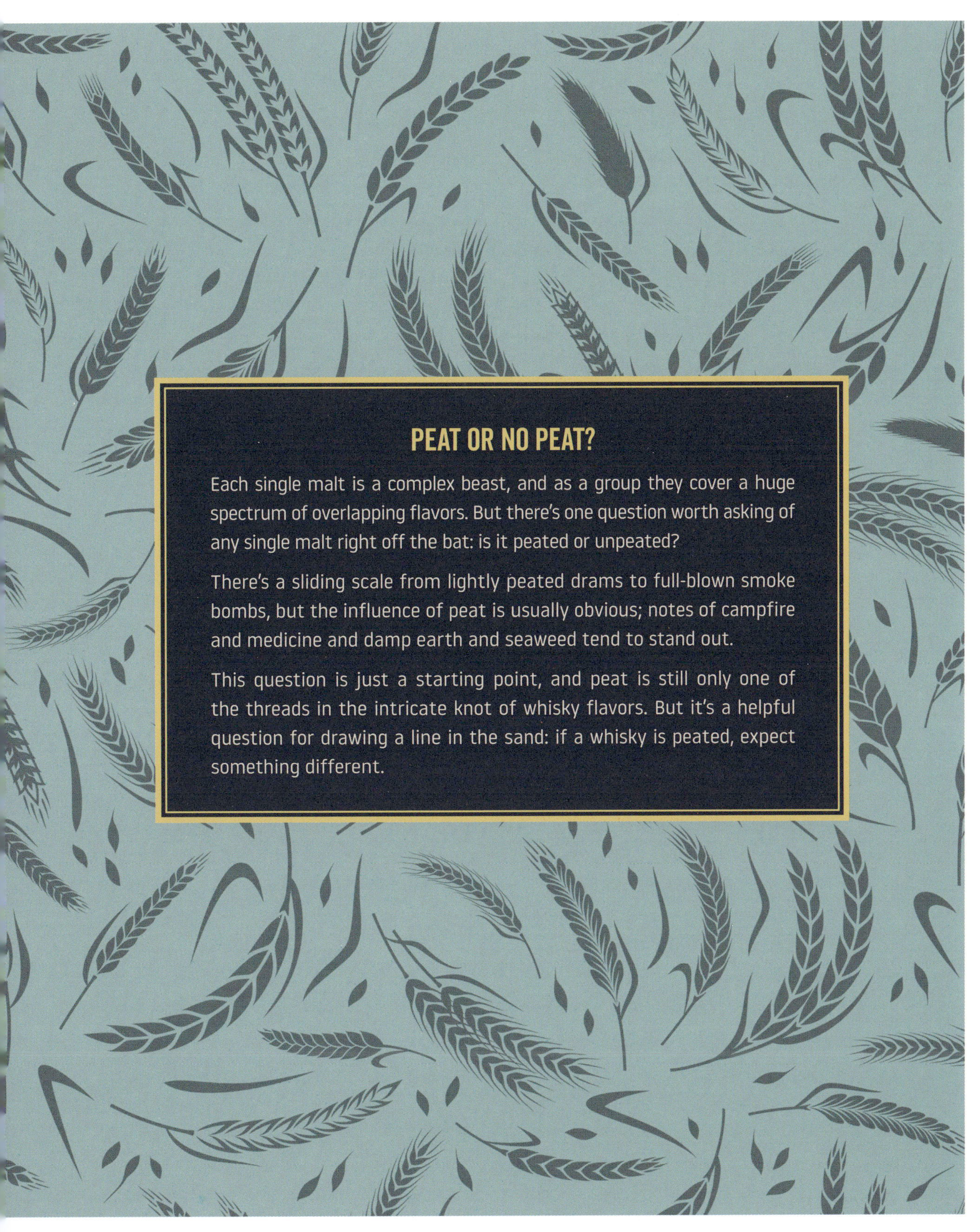

PEAT OR NO PEAT?

Each single malt is a complex beast, and as a group they cover a huge spectrum of overlapping flavors. But there's one question worth asking of any single malt right off the bat: is it peated or unpeated?

There's a sliding scale from lightly peated drams to full-blown smoke bombs, but the influence of peat is usually obvious; notes of campfire and medicine and damp earth and seaweed tend to stand out.

This question is just a starting point, and peat is still only one of the threads in the intricate knot of whisky flavors. But it's a helpful question for drawing a line in the sand: if a whisky is peated, expect something different.

Blended malt

A blended malt brings together several malt whiskies to sing in harmony, celebrating the depth and character of each one. It's like when famous pop singers form a supergroup – bring together some of the best in the biz, whose unique personalities and strengths complement each other, and watch them create beautiful music together.

Blended malts are far less common than single malts but keep an eye out for them – these supergroups make some number one hits.

Sometimes called "pure malt" (especially in Japan), or "world malt" if they contain whiskies from more than one country.

GRAIN WHISKY

Grain whisky covers all those whiskies that contain grains other than malted barley. (Confusing, considering barley is also a grain!) Most still contain some malt to help break down the sugars in the other grains, but you will find some whiskies made from 100% rye, wheat, or corn.

While malt whisky is made in pot stills, grain whisky can be made in column stills, giving more control over how pure the spirit is, and how much flavor carries over from the grain and fermentation.

There are huge industrial distilleries dedicated to making grain whisky for blending – its high alcohol and low character creates the perfect base for adding more flavorful whisky.

In Scotland, Ireland, and Japan, more distillers are exploring the flavor potential of grain whisky apart from blending, resulting in more single grain whisky being bottled than ever before, as well as the less common blended grain whisky.

America's the master of this category, with bourbon and rye whiskey leading the way. Compared to their grain whisky cousins across the pond, these Yanks have big personalities: they're loud, they're proud, with flavor they're well-endowed.

MASH BILLS

You don't have to be around bourbon or rye whiskey very long before you start hearing about mash bills. They're essentially the ingredients list of a whiskey, listing the proportions of each grain as a percentage: one bourbon might be 65% corn, 30% rye, 5% barley, while another is 75% corn, 13% rye, 12% barley.

Mash bills affect the balance of flavors in a whiskey, but they aren't the be-all and end-all – other ingredients and processes each play their part, too.

Bourbon

Once upon a time, bourbon was relegated to being the brown drink of the South. But over time, it's come to be appreciated as a quality spirit around America and around the world.

While it's still popular for mixing with cola and using in cocktails, there are more high-end expressions made for sophisticated sipping than ever before. Perhaps this classiness is thanks to bourbon's royal connection; its name comes from Bourbon County in Kentucky, which takes its name from the French House of Bourbon.

Most bourbon's made in Kentucky, with its abundant corn, limestone-filtered water, and variable climate. But there are distillers from Washington to Maine to Texas bringing diversity to the style with their different climates, different yeast strains, and even different varieties of corn.

Bourbon hasn't become too big for its boots . . . but it's given those boots a bit of a polish.

WHAT MAKES A BOURBON?

By law, bourbon must contain a minimum of 51% corn, though most sit up around the 70–75% mark. The remainder is made up of other grains; rye and malt are most common, but wheat's another option.

Like most American whiskeys, it's aged in new charred oak barrels. There's no minimum age for bourbon, but you won't be caught out – anything under four years is always declared on the label.

While bourbon has a strong association with Kentucky, it can be made anywhere in the United States. There are distillers in other countries making bourbon-style whisky – similar mash bills, methods, flavors – but they can't call their product bourbon.

It's standard for bourbon distillers to use the sour mash method, adding dregs of grain from one batch to the next to help fermentation. It's a science thing.

WHAT DOES IT TASTE LIKE?

More than many other whiskies: bourbon is sweet. The new oak and the corn both bring a sweetness that holds all the other flavors together. So while bourbons don't all taste the same, they do tend to bear a family resemblance: vanilla, caramel, and oak make up the bulk of bourbon's flavor profile, thanks again to the barrels.

But from here, each has its own personality shaped by the other ingredients and processes. The sweetness dial can be turned up or down depending on the percentage of corn used; the particular mash bill might deliver more spice or chocolate or nuttiness; a distillery's unique yeast strain might give off soft floral notes or rich dark fruit character; or their aging methods might bring out more honey or coconut or tobacco.

Even a small amount of rye in a mash bill adds complexity, but a high proportion of rye – 20–35% – will give an even bolder taste, flexing its spicy earthiness to balance out the sweet flavors.

Wheated bourbons bring a softer touch; wheat lets the oak and corn and malt do the talking while it provides a cushioning effect. These can be dessert in a glass.

Tennessee whiskey

Tennessee whiskey is . . . *very similar* to bourbon. It meets all the criteria of bourbon (minimum of 51% corn, aged in new charred oak barrels) but has a few extra requirements:

- It must be made in Tennessee.
- It's always aged for at least two years.
- It goes through the traditional Lincoln County Process, where the spirit is filtered through maple charcoal before going into barrels. This filtering gives a boost to the aging process, making the whiskey so smooth you could write songs about it.

Most of the world would call Tennessee whiskey a subset of bourbon; it's mainly people in Tennessee who'll insist on it being its own distinct style. And the best-selling American whiskey is consistently a Tennessee whiskey (Jack Daniel's), so they must be doing something right.

I'm just saying don't expect the flavors to be wildly different to bourbon.

Rye whiskey

Rye whiskey is bourbon's spunky older brother. The first American whiskeys, the fuel of the Revolution, the original spirit of the Manhattan and old fashioned cocktails – rye, rye, rye.

Once the most popular style in America, rye was all but extinguished by Prohibition. It's only since the 2000s that this style has picked itself up and dusted itself off – first as a cocktail ingredient, then as a drink enjoyed in its own right.

In turn, this has inspired distillers across the globe to explore rye whisky, even back in ol' Scotland (where it's classified as single grain whisky).

Strangely, Canadian whiskies picked up the nickname of "rye" somewhere along the way, regardless of their rye content . . . but putting aside that quirk of history, there are indeed Canadian whiskies made with a majority of rye.

WHAT MAKES A RYE?

American rye whiskey follows most of the same standards as bourbon – aged in new charred oak barrels, made anywhere in USA, etc – with the exception of the hero ingredient. It must contain a minimum of 51% rye, and a number of rye whiskeys stand firm at that minimum amount – rye is an intense grain! The rest of the mash bill is usually corn and barley.

But there are always people ready to push boundaries, and so there are rye whiskeys that use a higher proportion of rye, all the way up to 100% – that's a spicy meatball!

In other countries where rye is becoming popular, most distillers follow a similar path to the Americans, though they may put their own twist on the style with local grains or different casks.

WHAT DOES IT TASTE LIKE?

The word "spice" will always come up when talking about rye, but don't let your mind drift to a mouth-burning curry. Rye's spice can play out as peppercorns, cardamom, allspice, clove, cinnamon, nutmeg, or a peppery bite in the back of your throat.

A 51% rye whiskey will taste closer to a high-rye bourbon, with the corn and barrel sweetness tempering rye's sometimes aggressive nature.

As rye content pushes higher, so does the assertiveness of the grain, making the whiskey taste more dry, or even a little bitter. But there's a whole lot of complexity that comes along with the change, too – rye has an inherent fruitiness that really shines in high-rye whiskeys.

Don't be afraid – give rye a try.

Corn whiskey

Corn whiskey is bourbon's grandaddy. It doesn't follow the same rules as other American whiskeys: it must be over 80% corn, it doesn't have to be aged at all, and if it is aged, it will be in used or uncharred barrels. Geez, it's the Wild West all over again.

It's simple, sweet, and buttery, sometimes sprinkled with vanilla and spice. It's comfort food . . . but in a whiskey.

Wheat whiskey

Wheat whiskeys are a soft hug from strong arms. Made with a minimum 51% wheat, they're subtle and creamy; those with corn in the mash bill drink like a quieter bourbon, while those made of 100% wheat lean more toward wheat crackers with a light scraping of caramel and toffee.

If you like American whiskey and you like snuggling up in a warm blanket, wheat whiskey might be your thing.

American malt whiskey

Don't confuse this with single malt; these are whiskeys with at least 51% malted barley, other grains in the mash bill bringing their own character, and new charred oak slathering on its layers of vanilla, caramel, oak, and spice.

Single grain

In Scotland, Ireland, and Japan, there's always been a fair gap between the distinctive flavors of single malts and the milder character of blends. Single grains tend to sit in that gap.

As with single malts, the "single" here refers to a whisky being made in a single distillery. Single grain whisky can contain multiple kinds of grain, or even multiple grain whiskies that have been mixed together – as long as they're from the same distillery.

So while single malts must be made of 100% malt and made in a pot still, single grains have far more possibilities. Mostly wheat or corn with just a skerrick of malt, made in a column still? Rye whisky made in a pot still? Scotch made with 100% malt, distilled using a column still? All fair game for single grain. (Have I mentioned whisky categories are confusing?)

Many single grain whiskies are sweet, fruity, and characterful without being too intense. But of course, the flavors of any particular one will depend on a range of factors, including what grains it contains, how pure the spirit is distilled, and what casks are used for aging.

New waves of distillers are taking advantage of the wide scope of this category – and you should, too.

Blended grain

Grain whiskies from multiple distilleries blended together. Come on. You could have figured that out yourself.

BLENDED WHISKY

Blends are the bread and butter of the whisky industry. Single malt and bourbon may get more air time, but more blended whisky is drunk around the world than all other kinds of whisky combined.

The reason is simple: blends are crowdpleasers. In general, they're easy-drinking, appeal to a broad range of tastes, and are designed to play nice with mixers and in cocktails. And it doesn't hurt that they're cheaper than most other styles.

Like anything popular, blended whisky cops a lot of unfair criticism. Whisky snobs will accuse blends of being bland or say they're only for people who don't like whisky. And sure, there is a certain tier of blended whisky designed to be inoffensive rather than impressive.

But don't make the mistake of thinking subtle flavor means sub-par whisky. Skilled blenders are masters of their art, bringing the same expertise to blended whisky that they bring to world-class single malts. Each blend is a careful mix of different whiskies, batches, casks, ages, and flavors, with the end result being a spirit with more balance than a blind tightrope walker.

Blends are the friendly ushers that welcomed most of us to whisky in the first place and help people stick around long enough to fall in love with other styles. Some of the mass-produced blends may not be the most exciting whiskies on the shelf, but they definitely do belong on the shelf.

And don't let all this talk about the mainstream blends distract us from the fact that there are some truly, truly excellent blended whiskies out there.

WHAT MAKES A BLEND?

The exact rules and practices change from country to country, but the basic formula holds true: a lot of low-flavor whisky mixed with a smaller amount of high-flavor whisky.

Scotland, Ireland, and Japan have the same basic approach to blended whisky. You're looking at somewhere in the realm of 60–85% grain whisky (mostly wheat or corn) making up the base, with 15–40% malt whisky adding the flavor. Often it's just one grain whisky, but it could be any number of malt whiskies. Could be four. Could be 30.

In Canada, each grain is generally distilled and matured separately, giving blenders a huge range of spirits to work with. They start with a light and clean base whisky made of corn, then will season it with small amounts of more characterful whiskies: wheat and malted barley play their parts, but rye brings the most distinctive flavors to the table – . . . uh, bottle. Canadian distillers may use between 15 and 50 different whiskies in a blend and also have the unique option of a secret weapon: up to 9.09% of other flavoring like wine, port, sherry, or other spirits. That little rule blows the possibilities wide open.

Meanwhile, in the US, blended whiskey only has to contain a minimum of 20% American straight whiskey; the rest can be other whiskeys or neutral spirits. Yes, you read that right: 80% of a bottle of "American blended whiskey" *doesn't have to be whiskey*!

In all cases, a good blend is an artwork where the base whisky is the canvas, and the flavorful whiskies are the paints.

Or perhaps the grain whisky is a bass guitarist strumming gently in the background, while bolder flavored whiskies are the lead guitarist at the front of the stage, riffing on a double-necked axe.

I'm aware that I'm mixing metaphors. It seems appropriate here.

WHAT DOES IT TASTE LIKE?

The standard blends that make up most of the global whisky market are created to appeal to as many people as possible. These whiskies aren't going to blow you away, but they're also hard to hate. They're often described as "smooth" or "light", and will often have some combination of crisp fruitiness (like apple or pear), gentle sweetness (like vanilla or toffee), and a dusting of spice. They won't overpower your tastebuds . . . or perhaps I should say they won't overpower the mixer, because these are usually designed to mix well with cola or ginger ale.

Then there are premium blends, which are a totally different breed. They live by a different philosophy: flavor-driven rather than cost-driven. Premium blends are more adventurous, often weaving in more impactful or obscure or distinct whiskies to create layered flavor profiles you'd never find in standard blends. A syrupy ooze of tropical fruits, a smoky herbal concoction, a box of spiced cookies dipped in dark chocolate and sprinkled with orange zest . . . each one is an experience.

Japanese blends have a different feel again – closer to the premium end of the spectrum, but always extremely drinkable. Whether a particular blend is rich with honey or florals, stonefruit or citrus, butter or caramel, you'll always find it has a certain elegance.

OTHER

Pot still

Once upon a time, this unique Irish style made up the vast majority of whiskey in Ireland. Blends all but knocked pot still whiskey into oblivion, but it's back in the spotlight as more and more people want the taste of traditional Irish whiskey.

At a time when malted barley was taxed and unmalted barley wasn't, Irish distillers used a portion of unmalted barley in their whiskey as a way of paying less to the tax man (the goal of distillers everywhere). The whiskey they made was no longer single malt, but it was still made in a pot still – and the name stuck.

Pot still whiskey – or single pot still, when it's from a single distillery – must contain at least 30% malted barley and at least 30% unmalted barley and is allowed up to 5% other grains. The raw barley (often around half the mash bill) gives a full-bodied, almost creamy texture to pot still whiskey; bring this together with its nutty, spicy and grain-y notes, and pot still whiskey is like a plate of Nana's buttery biscuits.

Alternative grains

The velvety mouthfeel of oats. The toastiness of spelt. The grassy earthiness of buckwheat. The herbal undertones of quinoa. Distillers the world over are looking at the vast variety of grains available, looking at their distilling equipment, and thinking, "Why not . . . ?"

Sometimes they're returning to distilling traditions of days gone past. Sometimes they're using heirloom varieties that give their whisky a sense of place. Sometimes they're trying their hand at whatever wacky experimental grains they can get their hands on – and we get to be their guinea pigs.

Unaged / young spirit

Any distiller will tell you how important aging is in the whisky-making process . . . but some still like to give drinkers a sneak peek of the spirit before it's had its beauty sleep.

Some of this whisky-to-be is completely unaged – the new make spirit, bottled just as it is off the still. This clear, often slightly fruity spirit may be labeled as white malt spirit, moonshine, poitín/poteen, or white dog.

Sometimes a distiller decides a spirit is good to drink before it's reached the legal minimum age to be called whisky; they may label it as malt spirit, or "rye", or similar.

Then there are companies trying to speed up the aging process, experimenting with different sizes and shapes of wooden vessels, or forced temperature changes. Can you get the flavor of a 10-year-old whisky in three years? How about six weeks? Only one way to find out . . .

Flavored whiskies and liqueurs

There's an ever increasing number of flavored whiskies on the market. Most pull in flavors from within whisky's wheelhouse, like cinnamon, honey, maple syrup, or vanilla. But there are also bottles flavored with peanut butter, cookie dough, peach, and pumpkin spice. Nothing is sacred.

Whisky liqueurs seem like a bastardization of the glorious spirit, but people have been mixing whisky with honey, herbs, spices, and fruits for a very long time. If you have a sweet tooth, don't let anyone stop you from enjoying the silky decadence of Baileys Irish Cream, the fruity flamboyance of Southern Comfort, or the warming honey-and-herbs of Drambuie. Heck, you can double down by pouring them over ice cream.

WHISKY REGIONS

Just like people, each whisky is a product of its environment. No two countries have the same history, geography, climate, culture or distilling traditions, and so no two countries make whisky exactly the same way.

The five traditional whisky regions are Scotland, Ireland, USA, Canada, and Japan – places with long-standing whisky industries that export around the world. There are a lot of other countries making whisky, but since they don't have the same global reach, they tend to get lumped together and called "world whisky."

SCOTLAND

The location

You hear whisky, you think Scotland. You hear Scotland, you think whisky. Not surprising, since more scotch whisky is drunk around the world than all the American, Irish, and Japanese whisky combined. As I write these words, there are over 150 distilleries in Scotland, with around 12 billion bottles' worth of whisky maturing in warehouses. That's a lotta hooch.

Scotland and whisky have stuck together through good times and bad: from monks making medicine and farmers making firewater, through eras of moonshiners and bootleggers, to gaining respectability and growing into a booming export industry.

Scotland entered the 20th century with around 160 distilleries, but by 1933, all but 15 distilleries had closed. The industry had rebuilt by the 1970s . . . then crashed again in the '80s.

Thankfully, Scots are scrappy fighters. It's taken tenacity, corporate takeovers, and a helluva lot of marketing, but scotch has clawed its way back into bars and liquor cabinets and is now available in almost every country in the world.

Scotland is divided into five whisky-making regions: Highland, Lowland, Speyside, Islay, Campbeltown.

Of all the scotch regions, **Highland** has the largest footprint, stretching from the country's waistline right up to the north coast (not counting Speyside's roped-off area), and including all of Scotland's islands apart from Islay.

Nestled within the eastern shoulder of the Highlands, **Speyside** has always been a distiller's dream: an abundance of soft water, easy access to barley, and uninviting terrain that kept the tax men at bay.

Most of Scotland's grain whisky comes from six **Lowland** distilleries, making up the lion's share of blended scotch. Back when northern distillers were dodging the authorities, those in the south were quicker to play by the rules. They went legit and built large-scale distilleries to make whisky by the boatload – specifically, more approachable whisky that appealed to the cityfolk of Glasgow and Edinburgh.

Once, **Campbeltown** was called Whisky City, with 30-plus distilleries and a thriving export trade. Now it's called the "Wee Toon" reduced to just three distilleries on the small peninsula. (Though as I write, there are a few more on the horizon.)

Pronounced eye-la, not izz-lay, **Islay** stands defiantly against the Atlantic Ocean off Scotland's west coast. It's an island soaked by the sea – on the land, half-decayed marine plants form miles of peat bogs; in the air, sea spray invades the warehouses that hold whisky barrels.

The islands (other than Islay) are sometimes treated as an unofficial sixth region. If anything, their distilleries share most in common with those on Islay, being physically isolated from the mainland and often embracing peat smoke and salty notes. But officially, the islands belong to the Highlands. It's hard to beat a good rhyme.

The liquids

It's an understatement to say Scotland takes their whisky seriously. To be labeled as scotch, whisky must: be made and matured in Scotland; be made of grains, yeast, and water (a small amount of caramel color is allowed); be matured in oak casks for at least three years. If it don't fit this, it ain't scotch.

There are five kinds of whisky nestled under the scotch umbrella – single malt, blended malt, single grain, blended grain, and blended scotch – but the two big ones are blended scotch and single malt.

Blended whisky outstrips the other styles by miles, accounting for about three-quarters of all scotch. **Johnnie Walker** makes up the largest piece of this pie, celebrating malt whiskies from the four corners of Scotland in their blends; their Red Label boasts whisky from 35 distilleries. However, **Famous Grouse** is the favorite for Scots – perhaps because it uses some of Scotland's highest regarded malts, or perhaps because it's still Scottish-owned. **Compass Box** builds flavor profiles from the ground up, producing boundary-pushing blends like the patisserie-inspired Nectarosity.

However, it's single malts that dominate the conversation. There are more Scottish single malts than there are Pokémon (please don't fact check me on this), and they cover a huge spectrum of flavors since each is shaped by countless variables in ingredients and process.

Each bottle of single malt proudly announces what region it hails from . . . but don't expect that to tell you much about the liquid. These regions and their boundaries were set by politics and taxes, not what their whisky tastes like.

In ye olde days, there were more practical factors that could cause distilleries in an area to share a regional flavor. But nowadays, distillers can access knowledge and ingredients from everywhere, so there's far more diversity of styles. Taste two Speyside or Highland single malts at random, and chances are they'll taste nothing alike.

Highland's landscape varies from the rugged coasts to the sheltered inland, from the peak of Ben Nevis to the depths of Loch Ness, from peat bogs to pine forests to moors covered in heather – and its distilleries, spread far and wide, are just as diverse. At **Glenmorangie** (rhymes with "orange-y"), they boast stills as tall as giraffes (literally), elegant spirit with a citrussy twist, and an ongoing obsession with finishing whiskies in exotic casks. **Dalmore** is known for the silver stag head on its bottles, the ruddy glow of sherry-aged whisky, and a signature malt that's robust enough to hold up to a cigar. Then there are the islands: on Orkney, **Highland Park**'s honeyed heather sweetness is wrapped up in delicate tendrils of smoke, while on Skye, **Talisker**'s combination of sea spray, citrus and peppery smoky is like kissing a sea captain (in a good way).

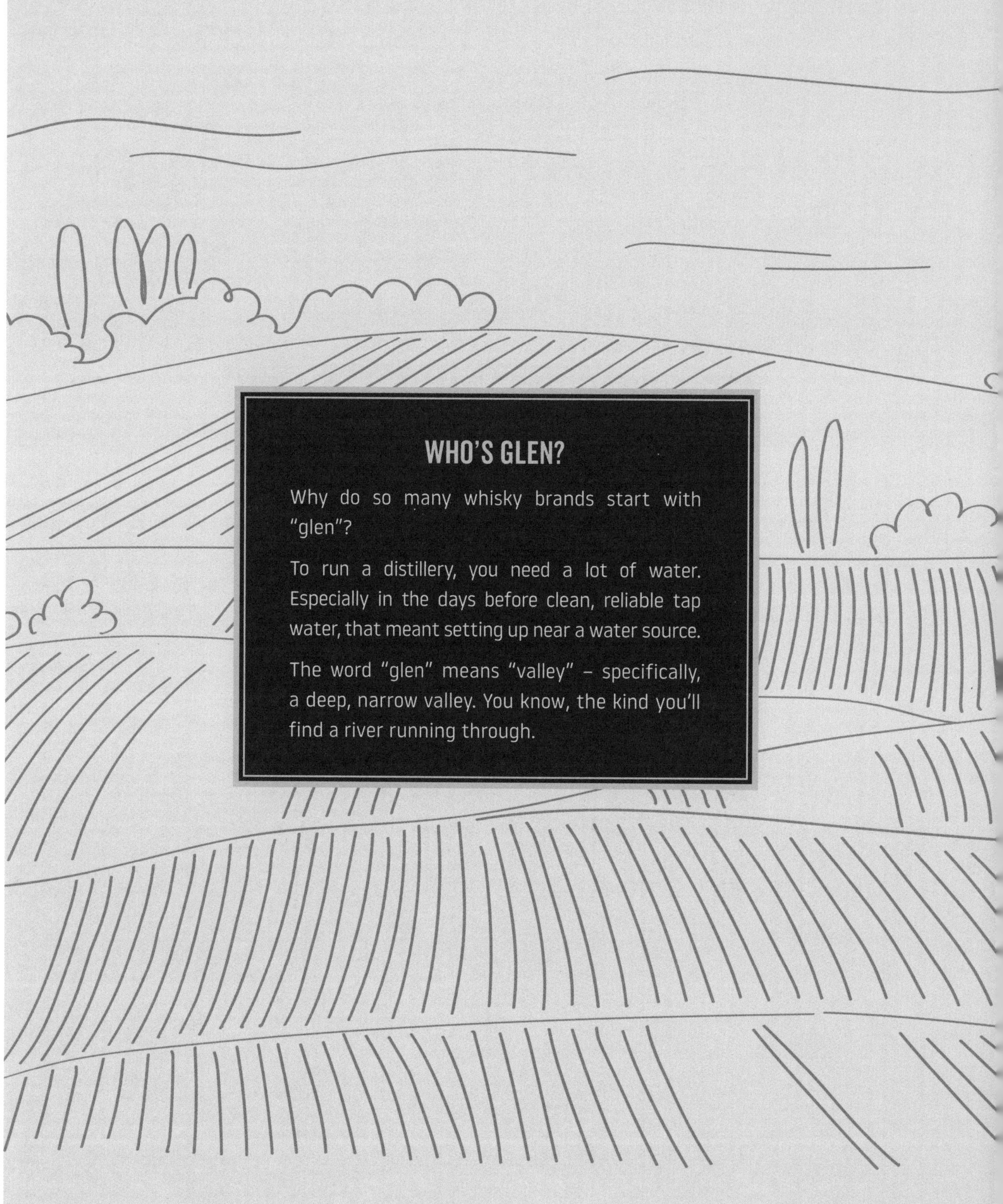

WHO'S GLEN?

Why do so many whisky brands start with "glen"?

To run a distillery, you need a lot of water. Especially in the days before clean, reliable tap water, that meant setting up near a water source.

The word "glen" means "valley" – specifically, a deep, narrow valley. You know, the kind you'll find a river running through.

You can't swing a unicorn in **Speyside** without hitting a distillery. But even though they're packed in tight, they offer up whiskies for every taste: from the light 'n' laidback **Glenfiddich**, the best-selling single malt that drinks like a frolic through the orchard; to the ruby-hued fruitcake-imbued **Glenfarclas** offerings; to the hearty roast-dinner-and-apple-strudel that is **Craigellachie**.

Lowland whiskies, on the other hand, are more akin to pre-dinner delicacies. **Auchentoshan**'s triple distillation makes it an outlier among scotch distilleries, and its easygoing drams are light and grassy with crisp, fresh fruit. The region's newer malt distilleries like **Bladnoch** bring an injection of energy but still respect Lowland's reputation for delicate flavors.

Campbeltown's whiskies are highly sought after, partly for their intriguing "Campbeltown funk": notes of brine, overripe fruit, machine oil, and wet sacks. Maybe it's the ocean air. Maybe it's the old equipment and hand-me-down distilling methods. But wherever it comes from, people want the funk.

Springbank has been owned by one family for 200 years – longer than any other distillery in Scotland – and they malt, mature, and bottle onsite. Revived after 85 years of being defunct, **Glengyle** releases single malts under the name Kilkerran, somehow spanning sweet, peaty, citrussy, salty, oily, and damp flavors. **Glen Scotia** is one of Scotland's smallest distilleries, and even after 200 years, it still wins awards; newer isn't always better.

Islay is small. Islay whiskies are not. Most of its distilleries lean into the maritime influence of the location, using oceanic peat and salt-soaked casks to make single malts that ooze smoke, sea salt, iodine, and seaweed. **Lagavulin** is viscous in texture and unapologetically pungent. **Laphroaig** has a medicinal whiff that, according to legend, is the reason it got a special exemption to keep flowing into the US during Prohibition. Not every Islay whisky tastes like a sailor's tobacco pipe. **Bruichladdich** has a number of unpeated whiskies that champion local and sustainable barley, and the nuances of flavor it can provide . . . though the same distillery also makes Octomore, the biggest baddest peat beast there is.

IRELAND

The location

Ireland was there at whiskey's beginning over 500 years ago, and Irish whiskey was the most popular spirit in the world through the 1800s. But between then and now, Ireland's whiskey industry was almost snuffed out completely.

It was an Irish invention that almost did it – the column still. Irish distillers rejected this newfangled technology for a long time, claiming that whatever spirit it made, it wasn't whiskey. But this valiant defense of pot stills and traditional methods put them on the back foot while blended scotch raced ahead. Ireland eventually came around to column stills and blends, but it had a lot of ground to recover.

Irish whiskey faced dark days through the 20th century. Distillers across the island dropped like flies, until all that was left was a pair of giant companies who joined forces to survive.

Slowly, the Irish whiskey flame grew. On the world stage, the novelty of Irish coffee helped keep it alight in people's minds, as did the nostalgia of Irish pubs; even the TV show *Cheers* played its part.

Like a political party obsessed with a single issue, Irish whiskey was always focused on being "smooth," backed up with the catch-cry of being "triple-distilled." The marketing worked, and Irish whiskey – mostly Jameson – found a home in bars around the world.

Today, Irish whiskey is in a much brighter place. Remember when there were just two distilleries? Now there are over 50. A new generation of distillers has risen up to remind the world why Ireland belongs on the podium. Some are looking to their roots, reviving historical recipes and traditional methods. Others are charging ahead into new flavor territory, shattering stereotypes of what Irish whiskey is – and what it can be. Even the big distillers are embracing flavor profiles that go beyond just "smooth."

Ireland may be divided, but whiskey is one thing they can unite over.

The liquids

Blends still lead the way by a mile, and **Jameson** is still bigger than Finn McCool; alongside the smooth original (did I mention it's triple-distilled?) you'll find editions that have spent time in stout- and IPA-seasoned casks. **Bushmills** holds the fort at the northern end of the island, and has done for centuries; the Black Bush and Red Bush blends include a whopping 80% malt whiskey, giving them more character than most affordable blends.

The resurgence of pot still whiskey, the unique Irish style that marries together malted and unmalted barley, is a gift to the world. The behemoth Midleton Distillery (home of Jameson) makes some of the more well-known expressions, including the dried fruit, marzipan, and custardy coziness of **Redbreast** and the green-apple-and-citrussy-freshness of **Green Spot.** At the artisan end of the spectrum, **Dingle** combines the creamy texture of single pot still whisky with the sweet complexity of fortified wine casks; dried figs, toasted nuts, dark chocolate, and leather are wrapped up with a spicy bite of ginger and clove. **Method and Madness** is a micro distillery range within the macro Midleton; since Irish law doesn't limit distillers to using oak, M&M has released single pot still whiskies finished in maple wood, Japanese cedar, hickory, French and Japanese chestnut.

The Tyrconnell offers single malts finished in Madeira, port, and sherry casks; each fortified wine introduces its own layers of fruitiness and spice to a caramel base for some intriguing dessert vibes. **Connemara** is a rare example of peated Irish single malt, bringing a kiss of earthy smoke together with honey, vanilla, apple, and spice for a whiskey that stands apart yet is distinctly Irish. **Teeling** is a young distillery in Dublin, but the Teeling family is old distilling royalty; who better to bolster Ireland's reputation by making award-winning single malt . . . and single grain . . . and single pot still . . . and poitín . . .

If you still haven't found what you're looking for, there are also a few distillers experimenting with the use of oats, since they historically played a significant role in Irish whiskey. But for more discussion on those, you'll have to wait for the sequel – *Whisky & Cocktails 2: Not This A-Grain.*

USA

The location

Since the days of the pioneers, the story of America has included the story of American whiskey. The two have grown up together: from corn farmers chugging moonshine, to cowboys shootin' 25-cent bourbon, to connoisseurs sipping cask strength rye while riding a bald eagle. (I may be slightly fuzzy on the details.)

While its origins were obviously inherited from Scotland and Ireland, American whiskey has very much trodden its own path. Rather than revolving around barley, whiskey in the US is built mostly around corn and rye – corn because it's cheap and plentiful, rye because it packs a punch even in small quantities. Stateside distilling has a language of its own with hammer mills, doublers, thumpers and rick houses (all of which would be excellent names for professional wrestlers). Bourbon makers are juggling a barrage of flavors from their proprietary yeast strains, charred new American oak barrels, and rollercoaster warehouse temperatures – a totally different world to distillers in the UK. And when it comes to craft distillers – those entrepreneurs who'll put everything on the line for a chance to create something that's never been done before – the Land of Opportunity leads the way without a doubt.

The upshot of this is a ridiculous number of whiskeys and an ever-expanding diversity of flavor. You'll almost always taste a familiar vanilla and toasty sweetness – a defining characteristic of American whiskey thanks to the new charred oak. But each individual offering shows off its own balance of corn (sweet and buttery), rye (spicy and fruity), wheat (soft and sultry) and barley (nutty and grassy) – along with about 50 other factors that make each one taste distinct.

Really, it's a fool's errand trying to capture a whiskey industry this size in a few hundred words – I should just shut up and let you get to drinking. But for better or worse, I'm a fool, and I rarely shut up.

The liquids

I don't think it's a secret that bourbon is the dominant style. There are more barrels of bourbon in Kentucky than there are people, and hundreds more distilleries across the country churning out the stuff. **Jim Beam's** white label is a mixing bourbon for millions, but the brand's Double Oak makes for a more interesting drink on its own. The folk at **Woodford Reserve** boast about their extra-long fermentation, triple distillation through a trio of pot stills, and barrels made and charred at their own cooperage. The luscious **Maker's Mark** is a wheated bourbon that goes down easier than most, but there's nothing easy about hand-dipping tens of millions of bottles into red wax. **Four Roses** is renowned for mixing and matching two different mash bills (one much higher in rye) and five yeast strains that each produce their own signature flavors; with these 10 spirits to draw from, they can make bourbons for every occasion.

Technically a Tennessee whiskey, **Jack Daniel's** sells more bottles than any bourbon; its flagship is sweet and simple, but jump a few rungs to the fancier offerings for flavors like peach cobbler, tobacco, cherry syrup, and almonds.

After all but disappearing from the scene after Prohibition, rye whiskey is back with a vengeance. **Angel's Envy** manages to stuff a lot of sweet treats into each bottle of rye; some get maple syrup and pecan, some get gingerbread and toasted marshmallow, some get cookie dough and Nutella. **Wild Turkey**'s Rare Breed Rye is a dry, herbal, spicy and cask strength – and you should put it in a Manhattan as soon as you can. **WhistlePig**'s outdoorsy flavors can be divisive, but 15-year-old 100% rye whiskey finished in Vermont oak that was grown onsite? Hot damn.

American single malt is on the rise, as distillers take inspiration from Scotland but then shape something of their own. **Stranahan's** from Colorado is one of the earliest American single malts; its honey, dried fruits, and breakfast cereal notes are sprinkled with vanilla sugar from the new charred oak barrels. Oregon's **Westward** approaches whiskey making with a brewer's sensibility, experimenting with specialty malts and even finishing a few whiskeys in various beer barrels from local brewers. **Corsair** in Tennessee have a single malt that weaves together three kinds of smoke – cherrywood, beechwood, and peat – and have experimented with mash bills including quinoa, triticale, spelt, and buckwheat.

Corn and wheat whiskeys hover around the edges of the American whiskey scene. **Balcones** has a pot-distilled corn whiskey made with nothing but roasted blue corn and tender loving care; the four-year-old **Mellow Corn** is thick and sticky and simple; and

Georgia Moon comes in a mason jar that proudly declares “less than 30 days old,” like some kind of Bizarro whiskey.

Reservoir makes a 100% wheat whiskey that’s all buttery spice and mouth-coating caramel, but **Bernheim’s** 51% wheat whiskey is the standard to beat: not because it’s been around for longer than most, but because it’s melted vanilla ice cream sprinkled with cinnamon sugar.

Oh, and every release from **Michter’s** is driven by their “cost be damned!” philosophy; they’re all truly excellent.

CANADA

The location

They've been making whisky in Canada since before it was Canada. You need something to keep you warm in the Great White North.

I don't want to accuse anyone of schadenfreude, but Canadian distillers have thrived any time their southern neighbors have struggled. During the American Civil War, they were happy to help the Yanks keep their thirst in check. During Prohibition, a river of booze flowed over the border from Canada into the USA – 1000 bottles of Canadian Club every day, or so the story goes. After Prohibition, Canadian distillers bought up cheap equipment from defunct US distilleries, which helped them grow. And Canadian whisky has been wildly popular in the States ever since, rivaling American whiskey on its home turf.

Good thing Canadians are some of the friendliest people on earth – and that their whisky is just as jovial.

The liquids

They do things a bit differently up in the Great White North.

First, it's common for distillers to ferment, distill and age each grain on its own, creating a range of spirits they can combine in different proportions to finetune the flavors of their blends. They're like wizards mixing whisky potions: "A cauldron of corn for sweetness, a beaker of malt for fruitiness, a vial of rye for spice, and an eye of newt for extra zing." (Note: only the rarest Canadian whiskies contain eye of newt.)

Second, the name "rye" gets slung around as a name for Canadian whisky – even blends that only contain 10% rye. But there are a bunch of proper rye whiskies on the market, too.

Third, Canada has a bonkers rule that allows distillers to include up to 9.09% "flavoring" in their whisky; that's one-eleventh of the bottle that could be sherry, port, wine, or other spirits. (Or more newt eyes, I guess?) The only stipulation is that the whisky still has to taste like Canadian whisky . . . which is a weirdly vague caveat in itself.

Crown Royal and **Canadian Club** are two of the biggest names; their entry-level products are smooth operators best mixed with cola or ginger ale, but their higher-end offerings are seductive sippers dripping with baking spices and butterscotch.

Not all distillers take advantage of that 9.09% rule; **Alberta Premium** is known for its 100% rye whiskies, breaking the stereotype of light-flavored Canadian whisky with spicy chocolate and dark fruits, and **Lot 40** 100% rye is made in small batches in a copper pot still, stirring up cinnamon, brown sugar, and leather.

But there are also distillers making the most of their creative freedom. **Forty Creek**'s portfolio includes a whisky flavored with hand-foraged botanicals and another with Caribbean rum, while **Bearface** makes a whisky infused with wild mushrooms and another that's one-eleventh smoky mezcal from Oaxaca, Mexico. Or if you want something sweeter, Quebec's **Sortilège** mixes whisky with maple syrup, which is about as Canadian as you can get without riding a moose.

Scottish-sounding **Glenora** claims the title of first single malt distillery in North America, releasing Glen Breton in 2000 and inspiring other craft distillers to try their hand at Canadian single malts.

Wayne Gretzky even has his own line of whiskies and liqueurs; I guess he really stands by his words: "You miss 100% of the shots you don't take."

WORTS LIMITED
OPEN
SPORT
GALLERY
VIS
academic challenge
personal leadership
responsible citizenship
grades 4-8
VIS
Voice Intermediate School
50

NIKKA WHISKY
NIKKA WHISKY
NIKKA WHISKY
NIKKA WHISKY
NIKKA WHISKY

JAPAN

The location

In Scotland, Ireland, and America, whisky grew up and evolved organically over centuries. But Japanese whisky came into being when two men decided to build a whisky industry.

Shinjiro Torii, founder of Suntory, needed a distiller to help him open Japan's first whisky distillery. He hired Masataka Taketsuru, a chemist who'd studied whisky making in Scotland. In 1923, they opened Yamazaki; nine years later, Taketsuru left to open his own distillery, and Nikka was born. Today, Suntory and Nikka are still the two foundational pillars of Japan's whisky empire.

Japanese whisky began by adopting Scottish ways, but don't expect it to be a kilt-wearing clone; over a hundred years, it's more than forged its own identity.

In Scotland, each distillery tends to have a house style. But in Japan, each distillery has many house styles - a single distillery will use multiple yeast strains, different types of stills, and a variety of processes to make a diversity of brands and flavors under one roof.

In Scotland, companies often trade whiskies in order to create blends. In Japan, corporations will create blends entirely from whiskies they own. They may use whiskies made in one distillery, multiple Japanese distilleries, or sometimes even distilleries in other countries - but always owned by the same Japanese parent company. They keep it in the family.

Japan has always been a country that values artisanal attention to detail, technological precision, and aesthetic beauty. Its whisky brings these together with finesse.

The liquids

The Japanese industry largely mirrors Scotland in the styles of whisky it produces: blends make up the bulk, single malts tell the stories, grains offer a point of difference. In terms of flavor, though, these whiskies lean into the Japanese preference for subtlety and nuance.

Blends are at the heart of Japanese whisky, and there's nothing second-rate about them. **Toki** is explicitly designed to make the perfect highball, with its delicate green fruit, fresh herbs, and fragrant spices. **Hibiki's** higher-end blends offer layers of flowers and fruits, and their Mizunara oak aromas are reminiscent of temple incense. **Akashi** whisky is made by a Toji – a grand master of sake-making – who uses sake methods and Japanese Shochu casks to fuse old Japanese distilling traditions into modern whisky.

An array of single malts tell the story of different distilleries, with each brand exploring variations on a theme. **Yamazaki** has the bragging rights of being the oldest distillery in Japan; their flagship 12-year-old is Japan's most famous single malt, and you can even get a bottle of 55-year-old if you're willing to spend a million bucks at auction. Built in the north where the conditions are closer to Scotland, red-roofed **Yoichi** Distillery does capture something of the Scottish spirit – single malts that dance with peat smoke, embrace the salty air from Ishikari Bay, and take on the dried fruit notes of sherry casks. **Hakushu's** single malts seem to soak up the fairytale forests surrounding the distillery: fresh and green, earthy and oaky, with light smatterings of fruit and spice and smoke poking out from behind the trees.

Grain whisky is on the rise and opening up new doors for drinkers to peek behind. **Nikka** puts its old Coffey stills on display with its Coffey Grain and Coffey Malt offerings – both are silky and sweet, but one shows off sticky tropical fruits while the other has a spice-driven freshness.

REST OF THE WORLD

Scotland, Ireland, USA, Japan, Canada – these five traditional whisky regions have been making the good stuff for a long time. But they aren't five mafia families who control the world's supply of the Water of Life. Whisky's gone global.

There are hundreds of distilleries around the world producing great whisky, with more opening all the time. Some follow the traditions of other whisky regions, honoring their methods, styles, and flavors. Some take inspiration from these regions, then make use of their own local ingredients or distinctive climates to create whisky unique to their country. Some go wild and forge their own path.

There aren't enough pages in this book to explore the history, culture, and variety of whisky in every country, but here's a taster . . .

At the beginning of the 20th century, whisky making in **England** completely dried up. For a hundred years, there were no English whisky distilleries. Then there was one, creatively named **The English Distillery**, which ended the drought with traditional single malts to meet the tastes of traditional whisky drinkers. One distillery led to another, and another, and 50 more – many of which are distinctly untraditional. At **Circumstance Distillery**, they break too many rules to make single malts, taking more inspiration from brewers than other whisky makers: they ferment their barley, rye, wheat, and oat whiskies for weeks instead of days, using yeasts normally reserved for French saisons, Belgian abbey ales, German hefeweizens, English strong ales and honey meads.

Over the border, **Wales** also experienced a hundred years of silence before a handful of distilleries stepped onto the scene. **Penderyn** was the first, laying the groundwork for a light and fruity style of Welsh whisky, and is the largest, with three distillery sites. Among the others, one uses all Welsh barley, one distills in a shed next to a 600-year-old stone and thatch pub, one grinds its malt with a meat grinder . . . all normal things in the Land of Dragons.

In **France**, many distillers approach whisky from different angles than in other countries. With converted brandy stills, expertise in distilling eaux-de-vie from various fruits, and a deep appreciation for terroir and the importance of casks, makers bring all kinds of fresh perspectives: like **Distillerie des Menhirs**, the family with a hundred-year heritage of making apple cider brandy now makes 100% buckwheat whisky; or **Domaine des Hautes Glaces**, the farm distillery exploring the terroir of whisky by using organic barley, rye and spelt grown in the French Alps; or **Hepp**, a distillery finishing whiskies in Armagnac, cherry liquor, and plum brandy casks.

In **Denmark**, whisky producers hunt down new flavors by blending tradition and innovation. At **Stauning**, they floor-malt their own barley with a contraption they MacGyvered themselves, smoke their own malt with local peat and heather, and source casks that once held mezcal, tequila, and stout. At **Copenhagen Distillery**, they season their own casks with anything from house-made rum and gin to seaweed and deer blood.

Israel's first single malt only showed up on the scene in 2017, but that's long enough to make a mark. **Milk & Honey** is a kosher certified craft distillery shaping the landscape of Israeli whisky, with releases including a single malt matured by the Dead Sea – the lowest place on earth – and one finished in pomegranate wine casks.

India has grown into a powerhouse of whisky, making world-class single malts inspired by Scotland but shaped by extreme climates. In a country with a booming population and an ever-growing thirst, there's a huge market for cheap "whisky" that's a blend of unaged spirit (often molasses-based) seasoned with a little whisky for flavor. To the rest of the world, that's not whisky. But that was the only "whisky" made in India . . . until 2004. **Amrut** released India's first single malt; the distillery makes a range of zesty and complex whiskies using Indian barley and Scottish peated malt. **Paul John** ages a portion of their casks in an underground warehouse, which protects them from rollercoaster temperatures and allows for steadier maturation; a characteristic honeyed sweetness binds their single malts together, and even the peated whiskies are surprisingly easy sippers. Both **Rampur**'s and **Indri**'s whiskies are made at the feet of the Himalayas; both fill their floral and fruity spirits into a variety of bourbon, sherry, and wine casks from around the world; both end up with a veritable rainbow of flavors.

While **China** has long been dominated by baijiu, its whisky industry is picking up speed and will soon be unstoppable. Having released mainland China's first single malt in 2015, **Yantai Gisbelle Distillery** uses mineral-rich water from the nearby Kunyu Mountain and ages its whiskies in casks made from Mongolian oak and seasoned with the distillery's own apple cider.

Taiwan is the only country in the world that drinks more single malt than blended whisky, so it stands to reason they take it seriously. **Kavalan Distillery** took out Best Single Malt at the 2015 World Whiskies Awards, and the single cask releases in their Soloist series have been collecting international awards ever since. Subtropical, but by no means sub-par.

In **Australia**, distillers around the country make every style of whisky imaginable – and make up new styles. Tasmania's Scotland-esque climate and peat bogs inspire a culture of single malt distilleries: trailblazing **Lark** set the standard for many others that would follow, like **Sullivans Cove** with its world-topping single cask releases. But Australians like to do things their own way. **Starward** draws from the wisdom of craft brewers and winemakers to create red wine barrel-aged whiskies that are sipped neat, mixed in cocktails, and blended into frozen whisky slushies. **The Gospel** are known for their unique spirit made from 100% unmalted rye from a single farm: some flows between barrels in a Spanish-inspired Solera system; some becomes American-style straight rye whiskey; some draws flavor from casks wet with tawny, rum, or vermouth. **Highwayman** is the brainchild of an Islay-obsessed maniac with WHISKY tattooed across his knuckles: small batches of viscous whiskies with intense flavors, often including the one-two punch of peat smoke and cask strength.

New Zealand also feels strangely similar to Scotland in many ways. But the country's distillers make truly Kiwi whisky, from **Thomson** using New Zealand barley smoked with native Manuka wood, to **Waitui** aging a single malt in Manuka honey mead barrels, and **Pōkeno** exploring the sweet and creamy notes that Totara wood casks can offer.

In **Bolivia**, the team at **Andean Culture Distillery** make whiskies infused with the taste of their country. Rare Bolivian Royal Quinoa in the mash bill? Indigenous Amburana oak barrels? Casks seasoned with Singani, a Bolivian brandy? These create whisky that couldn't be made anywhere else.

In **South Africa**, the pool of whisky producers is small but deep. **James Sedgwick Distillery** was established in 1886; released their first whisky in 1977; won World's Best Blended Whisky in 2012 with their entry-level Three Ships; and won World's Best Grain Whisky in 2013 with their Bain's Cape Mountain whisky, made from South African yellow maize.

HOT WEATHER, YOUNG WHISKY

You won't see many 15-year-old whiskies from India, Taiwan, or Australia – and there's a good reason for that.

When a barrel of whisky warms up, the liquid soaks into the wood; when it cools down, it retreats out of the wood. Ups and downs in temperature speed up the process, like when you dunk a teabag vigorously in hot water. In mild Scotland, the stable temperature gives slow maturation and older whiskies. But in regions with intense, changeable climates, whiskies may reach their peak in three or four years rather than 12 or 15.

They also evaporate more quickly. In Scotland, barrels lose about 2% of their whisky each year, but in hotter regions they can lose five times as much. Leave a barrel of scotch for 20 years and it's still two-thirds full; leave a barrel of Kentucky bourbon or Indian single malt for 20 years, and it's empty.

Next time you see a four-year-old single malt from a hot region, snap it up. It's good to go.

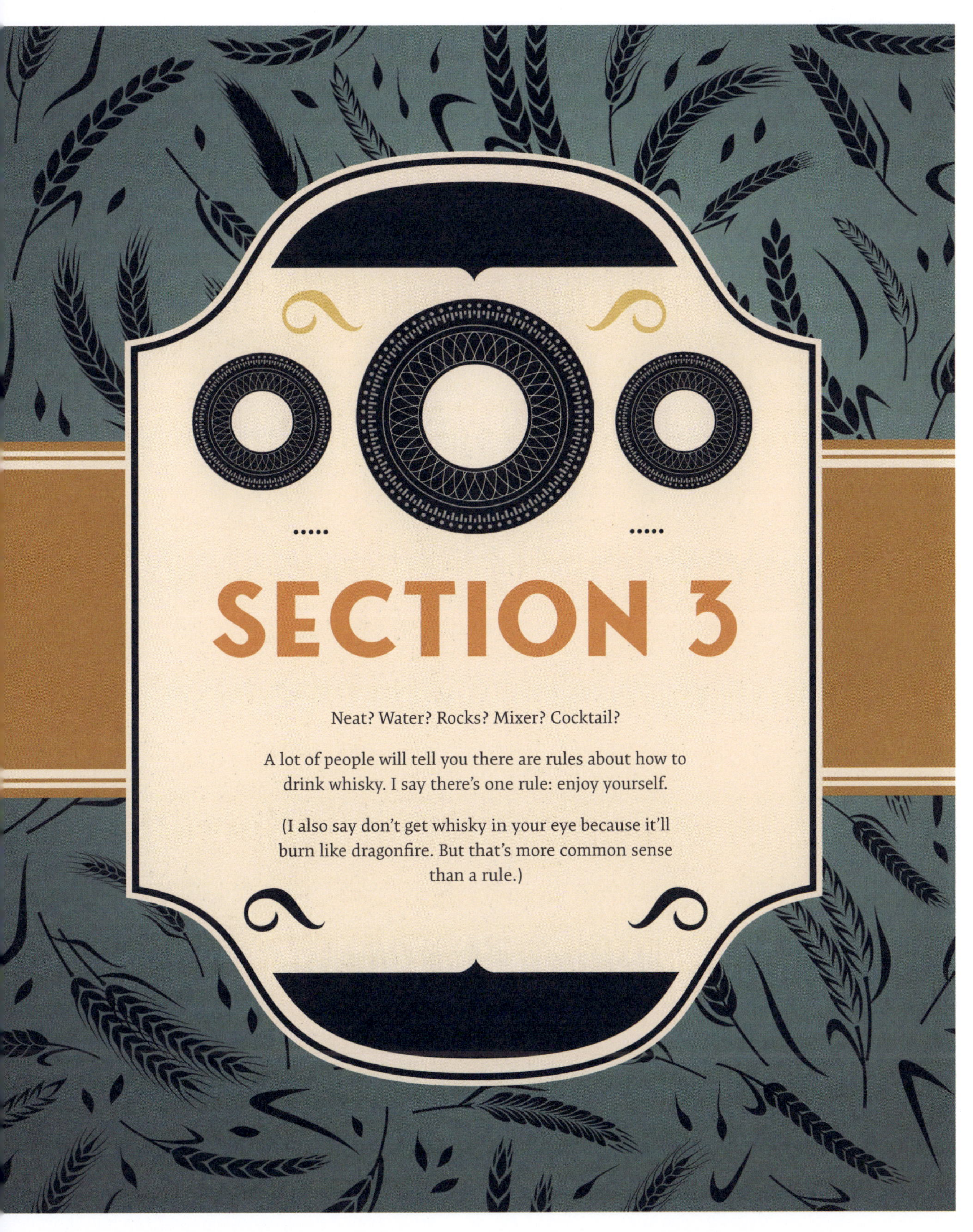

SECTION 3

Neat? Water? Rocks? Mixer? Cocktail?

A lot of people will tell you there are rules about how to drink whisky. I say there's one rule: enjoy yourself.

(I also say don't get whisky in your eye because it'll burn like dragonfire. But that's more common sense than a rule.)

TASTING WHISKY

To properly taste whisky, you need five identical polished glasses, a blindfold washed with scent-free soap, a sniffing trumpet to funnel aromas into the upper chambers of your nostrils . . .

No. No, you don't.

You need whisky, and you need a glass.

Sure, there are things that can enhance your experience, but a lack of paraphernalia shouldn't be a barrier to tasting whisky.

I'm going to walk you through an approach to tasting whisky that focuses on the most important equipment: your senses, your undivided attention, and a willingness to take your time. With this approach you'll notice aromas and flavors in a deeper way than when you're having a casual drink.

You don't need to drink this way all the time. (Your friends will stop inviting you out in public if you do.) But this way of tasting can help you . . .

- understand "whisky words"
- articulate what you like and don't like
- distinguish between different flavors and different kinds of whisky.

And next time you're reading labels in a store or talking to a bartender, choosing a whisky to drink neat or with a mixer or in a cocktail, you'll be better equipped to make that choice.

Ready to give it a go? Let's get tasting.

No sniffing trumpet required.

GETTING READY

Environment – you don't need a white room with no windows, but it's hard to focus on what you're tasting if the TV is blaring and the air is full of perfume or smoke.
Glass – a glass that narrows toward the rim can help concentrate the aromas. A tulip-shaped Glencairn is great; a curvy wine glass will do a similar job.
Pour size – a little goes a long way: ½ fl oz (15 ml) is enough to get a good sense of a whisky.

LOOK

Take a moment to gaze at your whisky like it's a painting in an art gallery. Hold it up to the light and watch it gleam like liquid gold. Give it a swirl and check out those sexy legs (the liquid that clings to the sides of the glass).

The appearance of a whisky won't tell you much about how it'll taste . . . but it's damn beautiful. Drink with your eyes first.

SMELL

Superhero, not sidekick

We often give our tastebuds all the credit when we enjoy food and drink, but that's not fair. Our experience of flavor is the combination of three senses – smell, taste, and feel – with smell doing around 75% of the work.

Smell is not an optional sidekick; it's the superhero that helps us discover all the goodness whisky has to offer. Give those aromas some attention.

Aromatics and alcohol fumes

Imagine there's a flower with a bee sitting on it. You want to smell the flower, but you don't want to inhale the bee and get a sting up your schnoz. Quite the conundrum.

Smelling whisky has the same issue. You want to breathe in the precious aromatics, but you don't want alcohol fumes burning your nostrils. They're not dangerous, but they can get in the way of delicate aromas – and they can sting!

Tips and techniques

A few techniques for smelling whisky without the burn:

- Long-distance sniffing – keep your nose away from the glass when you smell your whisky; find the sweet spot where you get aromas but not alcohol vapors.
- Drive-by sniffing – waft the glass under your nose and sniff the air above.
- Morse code sniffing – instead of long sniffs, take lots of short sniffs. You can even alternate nostrils.
- Mouth-smelling – hold the glass under your nose, but don't sniff; instead, inhale air in through your mouth. The aroma molecules rise into your nostrils, but the alcohol vapors don't. This is my favorite technique.

Dos and don'ts

- Do be patient. Wait a few minutes after pouring to let some of the vapors disperse.
- Do pause between sniffs. Give your nose a break, especially if it starts to sting.
- Do reset your sense of smell in between whiskies. Sniff the back of your hand or the inside of your elbow to wipe the slate clean.
- Don't stick your nose into the glass.
- Don't suck like a vacuum cleaner.
- Don't worry if you can only smell alcohol at first. Try again.

First and second impressions

Right up front: what does it smell like?

Don't overthink it – we're not looking for right or wrong answers. Just name any aromas you notice. You may only pick up one or two dominant notes at first: perhaps vanilla, caramel, honey, smoke, or even just a general sweetness or earthiness.

But that's just the first impression. You never get to know someone properly on the first date.

Have a break and breathe in some fresh air. When you come back, you often find the whisky's ready to share more of its personality. Warm spices? Fragrant fruit? Soft florals? Or even more distinct, familiar smells. Brown toast? Ripe stonefruit? The salty spray of the ocean upon a French bakery where the chocolate croissants are just starting to burn?

Smells can awaken memories and stir your creativity. There's no pressure to say fancy things, but feel free to let your mind go wherever the whisky takes you.

TASTE

Put it in your mouth.

The moment we've all been waiting for!

Start with a small sip, like it's a hot drink that'll burn if you gulp it.

This first taste may be a shock to the system, but you'll acclimatize quickly. Move the liquid around your mouth for a few seconds; swallow; take a few breaths.

Round two – take a larger sip. Let the whisky reach every part of your tongue, so all your tastebuds can join in. Suck in some air so your sense of smell can join the action, and breathe out some alcohol fumes.

Put your mind to work.

Focus on what you're tasting; you can even close your eyes.

What are your first impressions? Is the whisky sweet or dry? Smooth or sharp? Earthy or spicy? Do you taste vanilla, or caramel, or smoke, or fruit? Does it taste like it smelled, or unexpectedly different?

How does the liquid feel in your mouth? Is it thick or thin? Soft or harsh? Silky or oily or creamy or syrupy?

We've just looked at the big picture, but whisky is a photo mosaic; let's zoom in for a closer look and appreciate the smaller details.

Can you identify any individual flavor notes? Apple, or pear, or citrus? Honey, or toffee, or fudge? Coffee, or cocoa, or leather? Which flavors are front and center, and which ones are hiding at the edge? Do the flavors disappear after you've swallowed, or hang around like rebellious teens in a parking lot?

Some whiskies are smooth and balanced, so it's hard to pick out distinct flavor notes. Some are loud, with one or two flavors that shout in your face. Some are soft-spoken but reveal a wealth of flavors if you sit quietly with them.

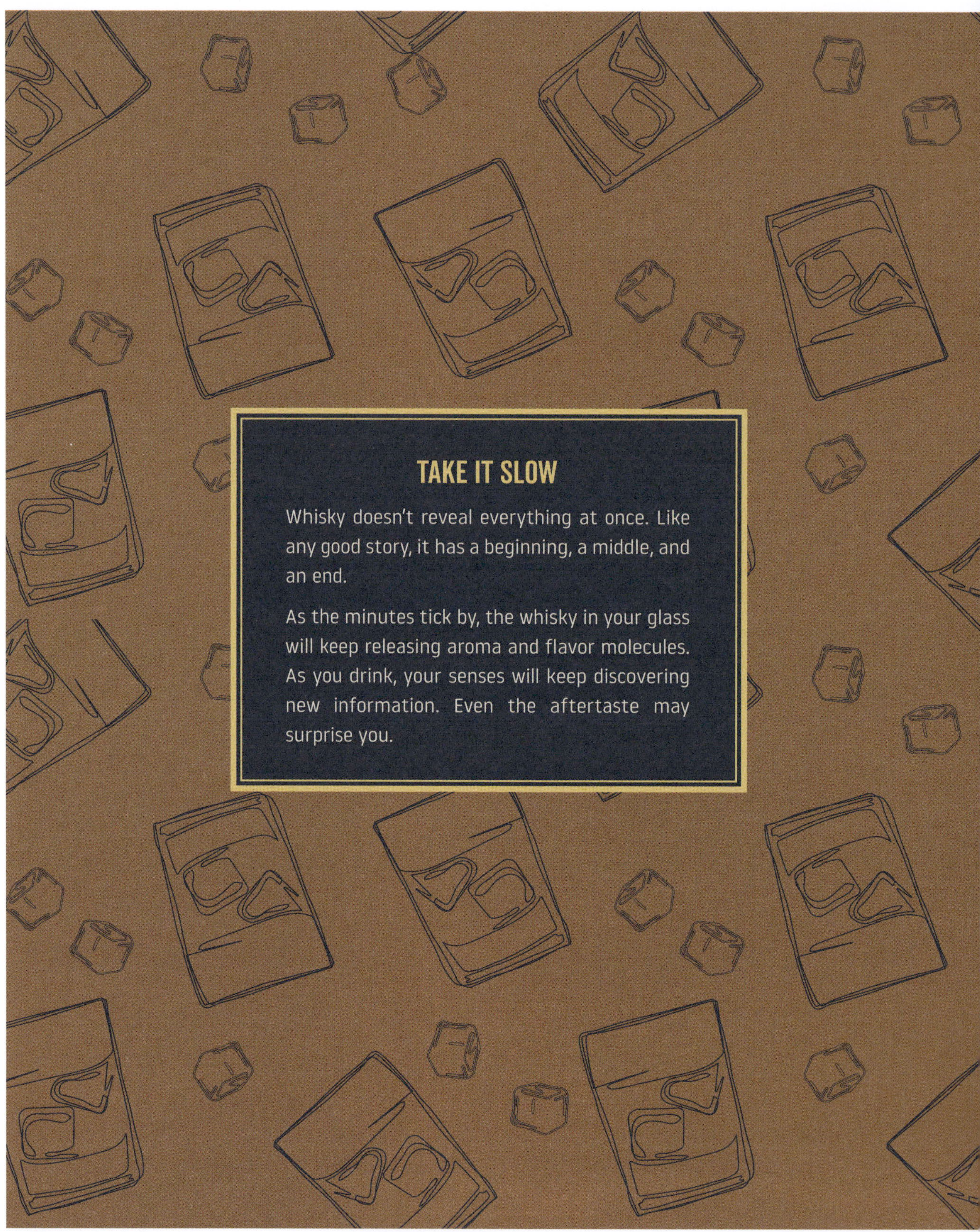

TAKE IT SLOW

Whisky doesn't reveal everything at once. Like any good story, it has a beginning, a middle, and an end.

As the minutes tick by, the whisky in your glass will keep releasing aroma and flavor molecules. As you drink, your senses will keep discovering new information. Even the aftertaste may surprise you.

Put it into words

Don't keep all those thoughts in your head – say them out loud.

Your brain is flooded with sensory data all the time, so it filters out anything that doesn't seem important. When you translate what you're smelling and tasting into words, your brain marks those aromas and flavors as "Important", and files them into your mental library.

Put some water in

Adding water can awaken new aromas and flavors in the whisky. It dilutes the alcohol, agitates the aroma molecules . . . recalibrates the jigawatts of the flux capacitor . . .

If you want to dig into the chemistry, ask a scientist. If you want to taste the difference, try it yourself.

Start with a few drops of room temperature water, then smell and taste again. The alcohol burn and bolder flavors will take a step back, allowing subtle and delicate notes to step forward. If you like, add a few more drops.

With some whiskies, a little water changes everything.

Put aside any insecurities.

Everyone's sense of smell and taste is different. You don't need to impress anyone by pretending to pick up notes of French mahogany and bumblebee fart.

Tasting whisky isn't a test, or a competition, or a job interview. It's a game with two players – you and your whisky – and you're on the same team. You can't lose.

So have fun playing!

THE FLAVORS OF WHISKY

Trying to list every flavor that might show up in whisky is like trying to count the stars. But here are some categories you can use as a guide. Start broad (e.g. floral, smoke) then try to narrow in on specific aromas and flavors (e.g. jasmine, bacon).

Light fruit & floral

green apple, pear, melon, fresh citrus, citrus blossom, jasmine, rose, honeysuckle, cut grass, fresh herbs

Rich fruit & nut

raisin, fig, date, stonefruit, banana, berry, marmalade, hazelnut, walnut, almond, Christmas cake

Sweet & grain

vanilla, caramel, honey, toffee, chocolate, coconut, butter, fudge, pastry, bread, biscuit, toast

Spice & wood

pepper, cinnamon, clove, nutmeg, liquorice, coffee, cocoa, wine, leather, oak

Smoke & peat

wood smoke, bacon, tobacco, sea spray, seaweed, iodine/medicinal, forest floor

Picking out flavor notes isn't always easy, but it's a skill that improves with practice. Keep at it – you'll be investing in a sniffing trumpet in no time.

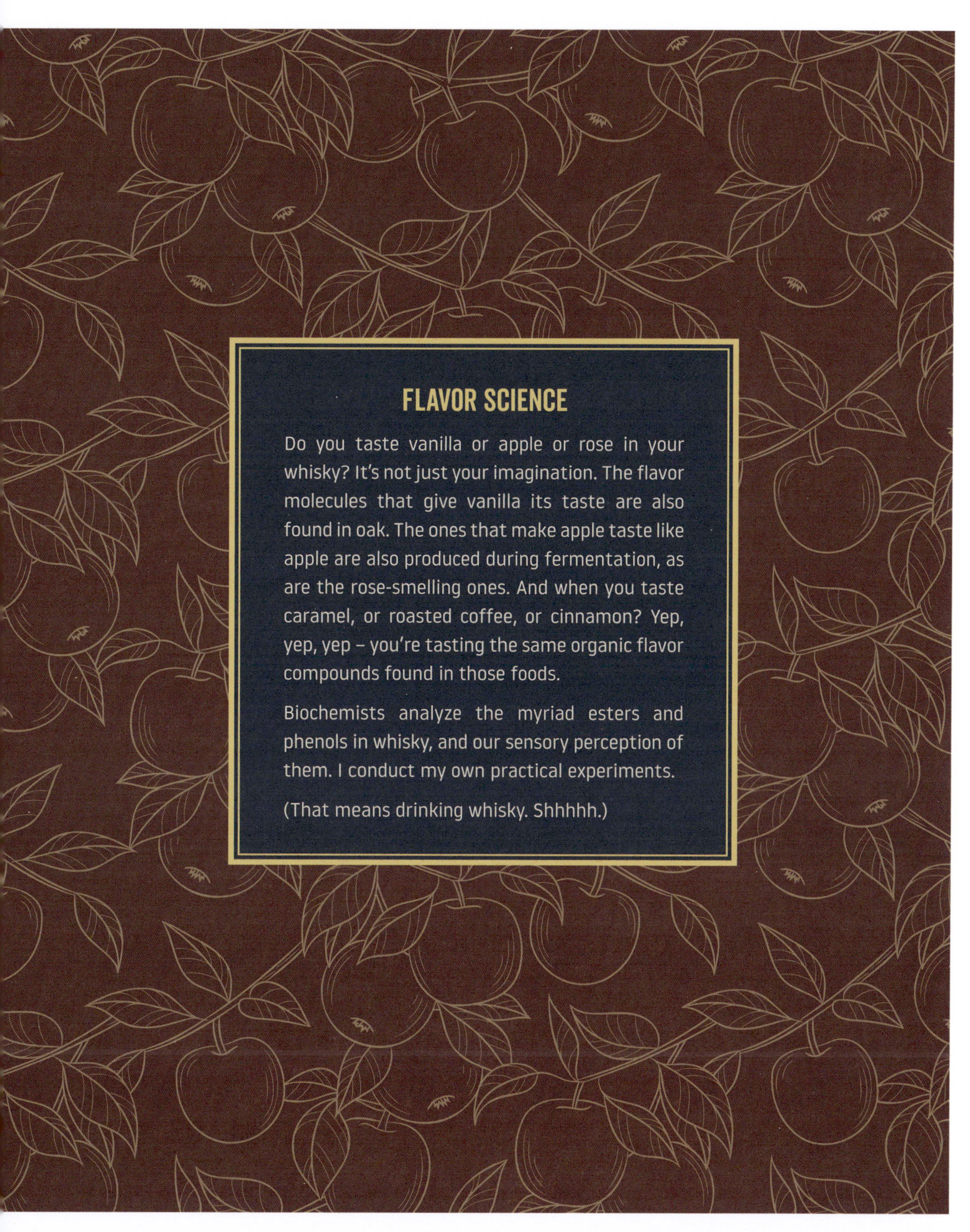

FLAVOR SCIENCE

Do you taste vanilla or apple or rose in your whisky? It's not just your imagination. The flavor molecules that give vanilla its taste are also found in oak. The ones that make apple taste like apple are also produced during fermentation, as are the rose-smelling ones. And when you taste caramel, or roasted coffee, or cinnamon? Yep, yep, yep – you're tasting the same organic flavor compounds found in those foods.

Biochemists analyze the myriad esters and phenols in whisky, and our sensory perception of them. I conduct my own practical experiments.

(That means drinking whisky. Shhhhh.)

WANT TO TAKE IT FURTHER?

Keen to hone yourself into a whisky tasting weapon?

Take notes. Your brain is the control hub for your senses – the more you engage it when you taste, the more attuned it will become at picking up nuances. Saying out loud what you smell and taste? Good. Writing them down? Better.

As a bonus, you'll end up with a record of the whiskies you've tasted. Your personal whisky encyclopedia!

Go beyond basic tasting notes. That blackberry flavor – is it fresh blackberries or blackberry jam? That vanilla flavor – is it custard or sponge cake? A nutty flavor could be roasted walnuts or sweet marzipan, and you might find that smoky flavor is more like smoked fish than a campfire.

Forget about "usual" tasting notes – you can go off script.

Specific is okay. ("It's chocolate, but not sweet creamy Cadbury . . . more like bitter dark chocolate sorbet.")

Combining flavors is okay. ("Mmm, this is almond biscotti dipped in espresso.")

Weird is okay. ("I'm getting band-aids, flower stems, and a camphor chest . . . and I like it!")

Personal associations and memories are okay. ("This smells like my grandfather's breath. He was always sucking butterscotch candies to cover the smell of cigars . . . ")

Feel free to get creative – it's all part of the fun.

Taste a whisky blind. If you can avoid spoilers from the label description and tasting notes, you'll push your palate to work harder. (You can read the label after making your own notes.)

Taste whiskies side-by-side. (Three or four at most – your poor tastebuds can only handle so much!) By comparing them and noting the similarities and differences, you'll pick up more subtleties than if you tasted them alone. Start with the lower ABV and lighter styles, and save any cask strength or peat monsters for the end; it's hard to appreciate a delicate piano solo when your ears are ringing from a heavy metal concert.

YOUR NOTES COULD INCLUDE . . .

What do you smell? (Beginning? Middle? End?)

What do you taste? (Beginning? Middle? End?)

Which aromas and flavors are dominant? Which are subtle?

How does the whisky feel in your mouth?

What changes when you add water?

What does this whisky remind you of?

What do you like/dislike about it?

How do you think it would go with soda water? With a mixer? In different cocktails?

SERVING UP YOUR WHISKY

THE GLASS

Hand someone a good-looking drink in a stylish glass and you'll make their day.

There are glasses that enhance the aromas of neat whisky, and glasses designed to suit certain cocktails. And there are glasses that just feel nice in your hand, like those crystal tumblers you find in second-hand shops.

It's good to know the options.

Glencairn

The tulip-shaped Glencairn is *the* glass for tasting whisky. A Scottish company designed it with input from master blenders to present the aromas and flavors of whisky in the best way.

The potbelly gives the whisky a wide surface area to release its aromatics, while the tapered mouth keeps those aromatics from floating away before your nose gets to them.

Very pretty. Very professional. Ideal for appreciating neat whisky. Not ideal for bourbon milkshakes.

Rocks / old fashioned / lowball

Different names, same basic glass shape: short and wide, usually cylindrical, often with a heavy base.

Like a decent pair of jeans, this versatile classic can be dressed up or down to suit the occasion. Whiskey sour? Scotch rocks? Bourbon 'n' coke? No problem. Even a Manhattan looks good in a lowball.

Curved or straight up-and-down? Patterned or plain? Dainty and delicate, or a heavy crystal brute you could use to fight off a mountain lion? You'll find the one that speaks to you.

(I've found three!)

Highball / Collins

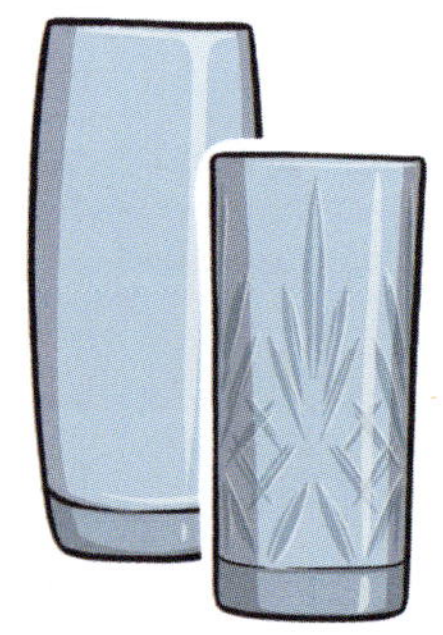

Technically these are different glasses, but they're used interchangeably. We're looking at a tall, narrow glass that helps fizzy drinks stay fizzy.

Whether you're crafting a perfect whisky highball or throwing together a mixed drink, this glass will keep 'em cold – it holds a lot of ice.

Also makes a good water glass when you're feeling fancy.

Shot glass

There is exactly one kind of person who should drink whisky from a shot glass. Unless you've got a slow drawl, a fast horse, a short temper, and a long-barrelled revolver, please don't do this to whisky. Or to yourself.

Martini, coupe, Nick & Nora

These glasses all do the same two things – they give you a stem to hold so your hand doesn't warm your cocktail, and they make you feel 33% more sophisticated.

Do you like angles and art deco? Go for a martini glass.

Prefer a curvaceous glass with a striking silhouette? You'll love the coupe.

Want to exude effortless cool and attract witty banter? Follow in the footsteps of Nick & Nora.

Copita

This sherry glass is for smelling, tasting, and appreciating the finer points of a whisky. Distillers and competition judges use it, but I reckon a Glencairn is less finicky and (slightly) less pretentious.

Quaich

This traditional two-handled drinking bowl has long been a symbol of hospitality and friendship in Scotland. You can't stab someone while you're drinking whisky with two hands.

Irish coffee glass

I'll give you three guesses what this one's for.

THE ICE

People have been obsessed with putting ice into drinks for two hundred years. (Ever read about the 19th century ice trade? Fascinating stuff!)

Ice doesn't just make drinks cold – it also affects their dilution, taste, and appearance. So let's learn from the *Titanic*'s mistakes and pay attention to ice.

(Too soon?)

Use clean-tasting ice

Ice can absorb odors from any open food in your freezer or fridge. Seal all your food into containers, or seal your ice into a container or ziplock bag. Or both, I guess.

Does the tap water where you live taste like chlorine, or dirt, or the inside of old metal pipes? Try making ice with filtered, distilled, or spring water for that clean, clean taste.

Start exploring larger ice

The larger your ice, the slower it melts – and it looks great in your glass, too.

Ice cube molds come in a range of shapes and sizes. Big cubes? Spheres? Erotic shapes that make your guests chuckle, then feel uncomfortable? Choose your favorite.

Hand-carved ice – how impressive!

Freeze a container of water to make a large block of ice. Use a knife (a cheap serrated bread knife works well) to saw a deep line all the way around, then break the ice along that line to create big, rustic rocks of ice. (Or just smash the ice and use the shards.)

Make ice that's more than just water

Do you drink whisky with a mixer? Freeze your mixer into ice cubes that won't make your drink taste watery.

Play around with freezing garnishes into ice cubes. Orange twist? Maraschino cherry? Tiny caveman fighting a woolly mammoth? So many options!

Discover gorgeous clear ice

Look at the ice cubes in your freezer. They've got that white cloudy stuff in the middle – air bubbles and impurities in the water.

Clear ice doesn't have these junk-bubbles. Not only does it look stunning, but it melts more slowly and has a purer taste than normal ice.

You can make clear ice using a method called directional freezing – encouraging ice cubes to freeze from only one side, which pushes out the bubbles and impurities.

I use an insulated travel mug: fill it with water, leave it in the freezer for 36 to 48 hours, then remove the ice and chop off the white bit at the bottom. You can also buy specialized ice molds that make clear ice.

Go down the rabbit hole by researching Camper English, who popularized directional freezing and started a clear ice movement.

WAYS OF DRINKING WHISKY

Everyone's got an opinion on how you should drink whisky:

"Only neat . . . "

"Only after the sun goes down . . . "

"Only in cold weather . . . "

To these people I say: Nope. Nae. *Ní aontaím.*

A neat whisky on a winter's night is sublime. Liquid firelight for the soul. But *only* neat? *Only* at night? *Only* in winter? Next you'll be saying I should only breathe air on Tuesdays and Thursdays.

Here's my opinion on how you should drink whisky: however you enjoy it. Whisky's fan-freaking-tastic in all its forms.

On its own, it's a precious gem to be appreciated from every angle.

With a mixer, it shares its excellence with whatever it touches.

In cocktails, it brings a complexity that blows vodka martinis out of the water.

We all have different tastes, and personal preference is everything. Drink what you like.

It's exciting to find new ways to enjoy whisky. So here's my second opinion: try whisky a bunch of different ways. It's fine to have a favorite drink, but there are all kinds of delights outside your comfort zone, just waiting for you to discover them.

NEAT (ON ITS OWN)

Au naturel. Naked. The way God intended.

This is the simplest way to serve and drink whisky: no water, no ice, no mixer, no nothing.

But simple doesn't mean simplistic. Whisky's a complex drink and drinking it in its purest form gives you the chance to discover all its nooks and crannies.

It's also a strong drink. Not just in alcohol; the flavors are full-on, too. When you drink it neat, it's just you and the whisky with nothing in between, staring each other down like Gandalf facing off against the Balrog. It's intense. But that intensity is what's so good about whisky!

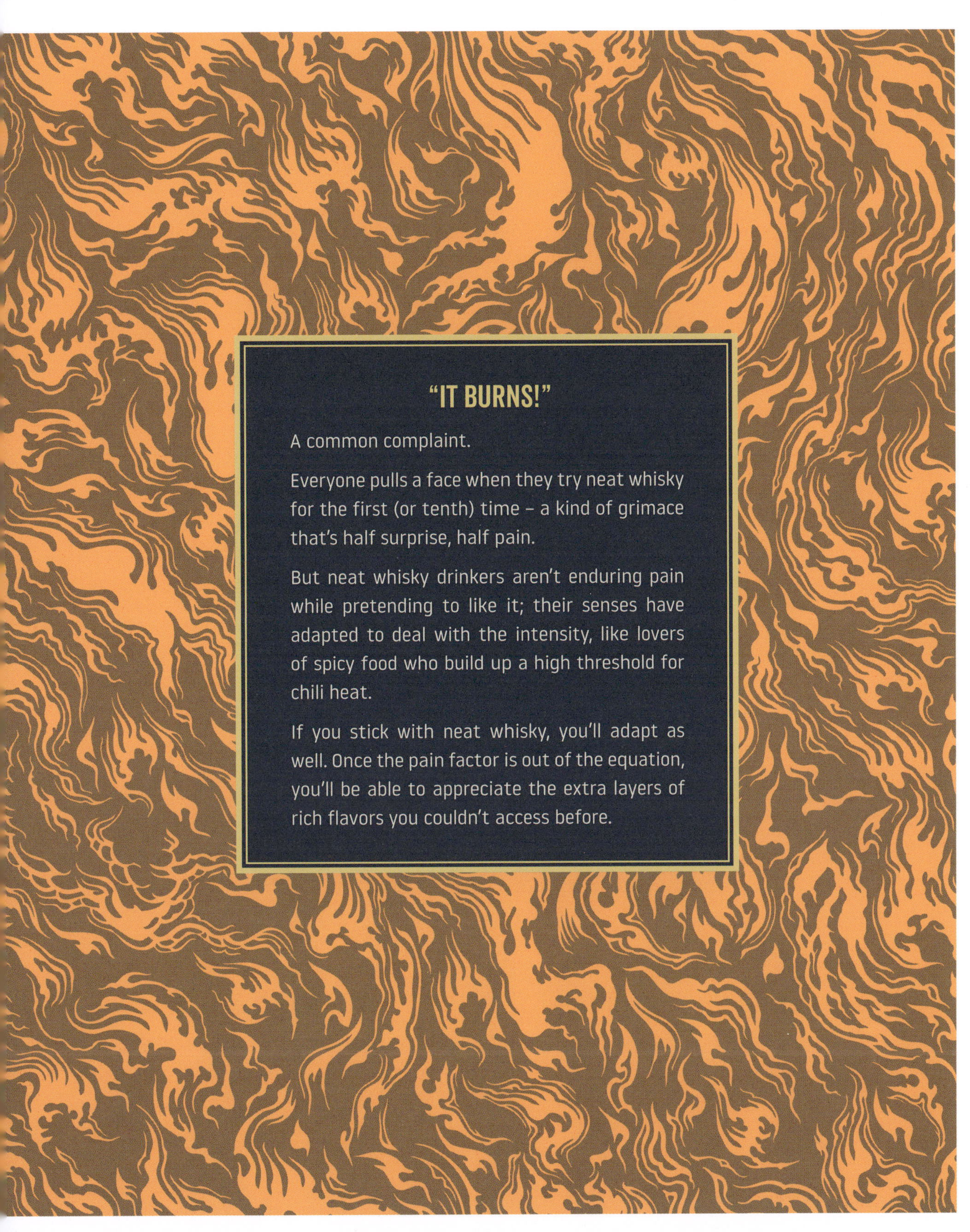

"IT BURNS!"

A common complaint.

Everyone pulls a face when they try neat whisky for the first (or tenth) time – a kind of grimace that's half surprise, half pain.

But neat whisky drinkers aren't enduring pain while pretending to like it; their senses have adapted to deal with the intensity, like lovers of spicy food who build up a high threshold for chili heat.

If you stick with neat whisky, you'll adapt as well. Once the pain factor is out of the equation, you'll be able to appreciate the extra layers of rich flavors you couldn't access before.

How much do you drink? Depending on where you live, ordering neat whisky in a bar could get you a pour anywhere between ¾ fl oz (25 ml) and 2 fl oz (60 ml).

If you're pouring for yourself at home, have exactly as much as you want. (And if you're like me, you're not measuring anyway.)

Or you might not pour it at all. I'm a big fan of sneaking a hip flask into the drive-in theater or taking a swig from the bottle when I open the pantry late at night the same way you sneak a bite of leftover pizza when you open the fridge. Who says neat whisky has to be sophisticated?

What whiskies can you drink neat? The short answer is: any whisky.

But the choice does matter. Some whiskies are better suited for neat sipping than others, especially according to your personal taste.

I wouldn't bother with the cheapest whisky around. Lower-end whiskies tend not to have a lot going on flavor-wise, and the whole point of neat whisky is to experience the flavors.

If you don't want to go too intense, look for descriptors like smooth, sweet, creamy, mild, light. Softer flavors such as apple or floral notes may imply a less aggressive character. Many Speyside and Highland single malts boast a honeyed profile, most bourbons are sweet thanks to the use of new oak, and many Japanese whiskies pride themselves on their delicate flavors.

If you're after bold and distinctive flavors, your options are wide open. Chase down a spicy rye or a fruity sherry cask finish. Islay single malts are often smoky, earthy, rugged, and other words that sound like a shirtless hunk in a cologne commercial. Irish pot still whiskey has a unique complexity from its use of unmalted barley. Drinking a cask strength whisky neat is like riding a wild stallion bareback: only for the brave of heart and may hurt sensitive parts of your body. (There's a reason people invented saddles.)

Every time I acquire a new whisky, I'll always try it neat first. I like to size it up, like it's a gunslinger challenging me to a duel at high noon. Once I've tasted the whisky, the whole whisky, and nothing but the whisky, I can decide whether I want to add water or make an old fashioned or pour it in my coffee – or keep drinking it neat.

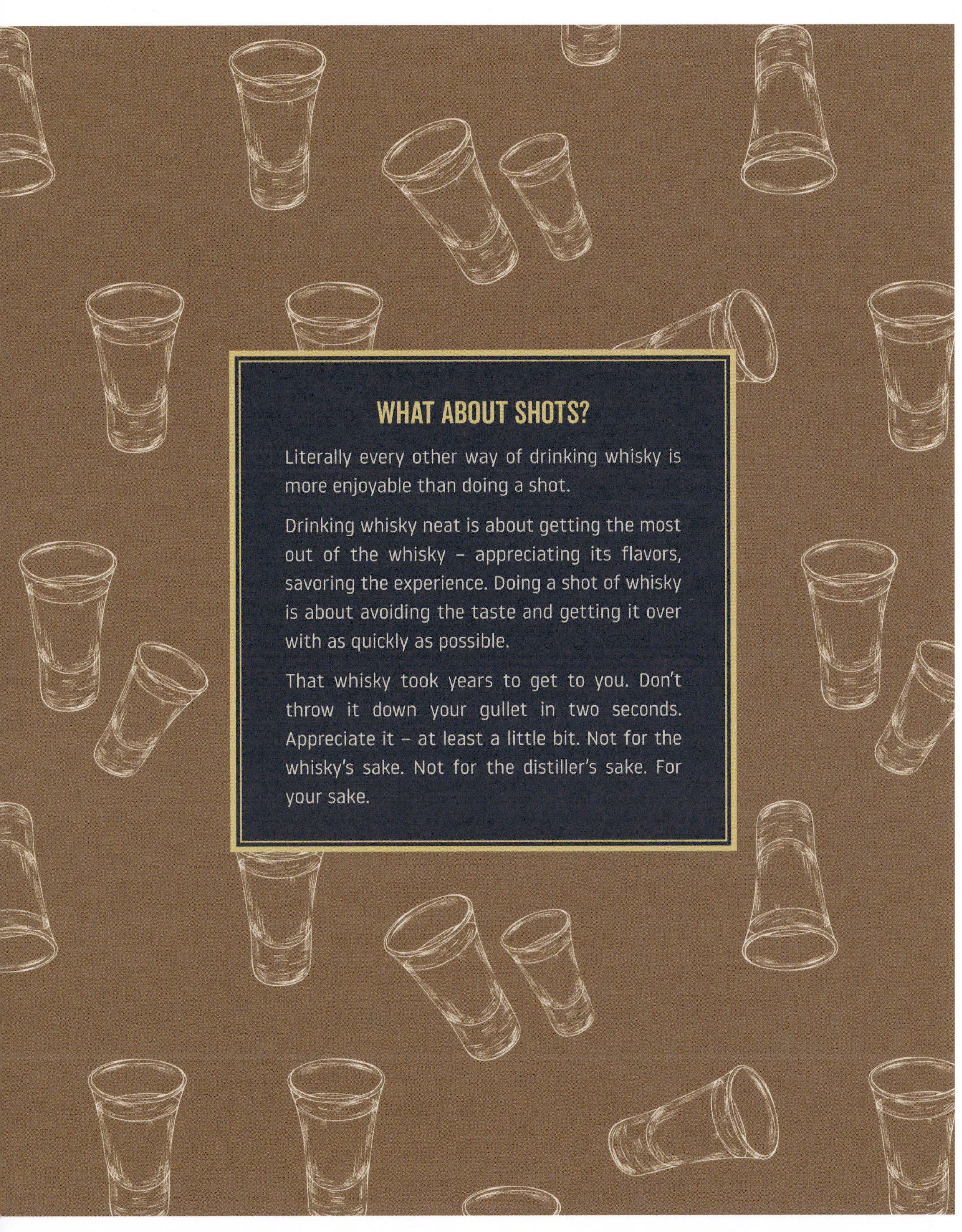

WHAT ABOUT SHOTS?

Literally every other way of drinking whisky is more enjoyable than doing a shot.

Drinking whisky neat is about getting the most out of the whisky – appreciating its flavors, savoring the experience. Doing a shot of whisky is about avoiding the taste and getting it over with as quickly as possible.

That whisky took years to get to you. Don't throw it down your gullet in two seconds. Appreciate it – at least a little bit. Not for the whisky's sake. Not for the distiller's sake. For your sake.

WITH WATER

Adding a little water to your whisky does two main things.

The first is simple: it dilutes the alcohol. In such a small volume of whisky, even a few drops of water can take the edge off, reducing the burn to your nose and mouth. With less heat from the booze, your tastebuds can pick up more of the subtle flavors; when you turn the bass down, you can hear the vocals more clearly.

The second is less intuitive: adding water to whisky changes the way it smells and tastes. It doesn't inject new flavors, but it unlocks aroma and flavor compounds that were trapped, making them available to your senses.

It can be surprising how different a whisky tastes with a bit of water added. It's still the same whisky, but you perceive it more clearly and appreciate it more, like when someone in a rom-com has a makeover montage.

Not *every* whisky improves with water; some heavily sherried single malts and some older whiskies can be better without. But for most whiskies, it's a good change.

- Always use clean-tasting water. Some people swear by spring water.
- Use room temperature water; cold can shut down the aromas and flavors.
- If you're in a bar, don't ask for a whisky and water. Order neat whisky with water on the side – no ice.
- Smell and taste the whisky on its own before adding any water. You might decide you don't want any after all.
- Start by adding just a few drops. If you're in a whisky bar, they may give you a water dropper. Or if you have a straw, you can use that. Or just use your fingers, like I do.
- How much water you should add depends on the whisky and your personal taste. Add a little at a time, tasting as you go, until you find your sweet spot.
- For many people, a few drops is enough. Some go all the way up to equal parts water and whisky. Japanese *mizuwari*-style can be up to four parts water to one part whisky!
- Take it slow. If you accidentally add too much, your glass of beautiful whisky will taste like water and regret. When this happens, there's no going back.
- Though there is one way forward: add more whisky!

ON THE ROCKS (WITH ICE)

Whisky on the rocks is an experience bigger than the liquid itself.

It's how most people drink whisky in movies and on TV. It feels cool to order whisky on the rocks at a bar. (No pun intended.) (Well, maybe a little pun intended.) And the clinking of ice cubes in a crystal tumbler is a sweeter sound than most music in existence.

But before you channel your favorite movie star, be aware: when you put ice in whisky, it turns the volume right down.

Remember how room temperature water wakes up those aroma and flavor compounds? Well, the sharp coldness of ice can put them to sleep. The cold can also numb your tastebuds so they're less sensitive to subtle flavors.

And the dilution from melting ice can turn your whisky into a bad version of Goldilocks: at first, it's still too strong; then, for a brief moment, it's just right . . . but then the ice keeps melting and your drink becomes too watery.

So if you want to explore all the complex flavors of whisky, ice is counterproductive.

But don't let this put you off drinking your whisky on the rocks when you want to.

Maybe it's summer and you're sweating like a pig – you want whisky, you want ice, and you expect it to last all of 60 seconds.

Maybe you do want to tone your whisky right down – no judgment here.

Maybe you've had a hard day and want an undemanding drink – you still want the vanilla-caramel of your bourbon, or a hit of spice and smoke from your scotch, but don't need much else right now.

Or maybe you just prefer it that way. You don't need to explain yourself to anyone.

How do you go about putting ice in whisky?

- Use a rocks glass. It's in the name.
- Use bigger pieces of ice to slow the melting. A single large cube that fills the glass is effective – and gorgeous.
- Appreciate the way the flavors evolve minute by minute as the ice melts.
- Swirl your glass. Clink your ice. Be cool.

If you want to taste the intricacies of a quality whisky, ice may not be the best way to go.

But if you want to chill your drink, switch off your brain, and feel like James Bond or Mila Kunis – go ahead and enjoy your whisky on the rocks.

GET STONED

I feel obligated to mention whisky stones. They're small cubes of stone – usually soapstone or granite – that you keep in the freezer, then add to your whisky to cool your drink without the dilution of melting ice.

Whisky stones are good at what they do . . . but they're not for me. I like a little water in my whisky, and I don't like being ever-vigilant about stones that might clack against my teeth.

SODA WATER (HIGHBALL)

People have been drinking whisky with soda water since the late 1800s. It's come in and out of fashion more times than baggy pants, but it's never gone away. And so it shouldn't! Bubbles are a satisfying addition to whisky, shaping how it hits our senses: they elevate the aromas, alter the mouthfeel, and stimulate our tastebuds.

The most basic version of whisky and soda is a lowball glass with a handful of ice, low-end whisky, topped up with cheap soda water. This is the order of grandfathers and no-nonsense drinkers. No muss, no fuss. Unpretentious. Uninspiring.

Then there's the leveled-up version: the whisky highball.

(Some people use the word "highball" to mean any combination of whisky + mixer. Here, I'm using the narrow definition of whisky + soda water.)

Highballs aren't a recent invention – a cocktail book from 1895 includes a highball recipe – but the whisky renaissance has brought them back into the spotlight.

A well-made highball hits all the senses. The beauty of this drink is in the details: the glass, the ice, the choice of whisky, the quality of soda water, the method. In a nice bar, you'll get a highball glass filled with clean ice cubes, your whisky of choice, and a top-up from a small bottle of soda water. Citrus twist optional (but recommended). Low effort. Casual but classy. Delicious.

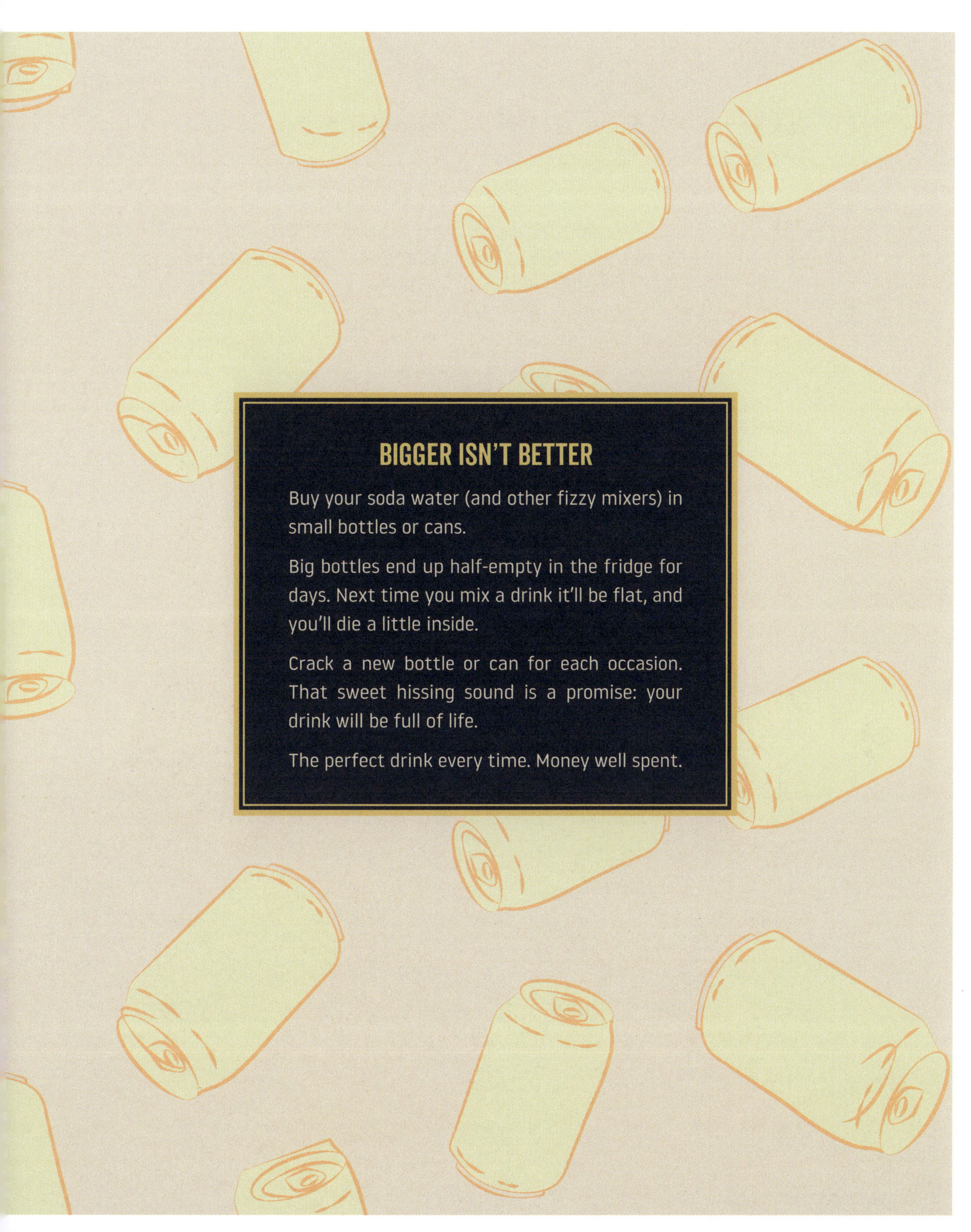

BIGGER ISN'T BETTER

Buy your soda water (and other fizzy mixers) in small bottles or cans.

Big bottles end up half-empty in the fridge for days. Next time you mix a drink it'll be flat, and you'll die a little inside.

Crack a new bottle or can for each occasion. That sweet hissing sound is a promise: your drink will be full of life.

The perfect drink every time. Money well spent.

Highballs evolved again in the 2000s thanks to the influence of Japanese bartenders. Enter the deluxe version: "Japanese whisky highball."

As highballs became popular in Japan, passionate bartenders elevated it to an art form. By obsessing over everything – effervescence, temperature, dilution – they turned something ordinary into something extraordinary. An elegant highball glass, chilled and filled with two hand-carved blocks of clear ice stacked on top of each other; a fragrant whisky selected for the way it shines in a highball; a carefully chosen premium sparkling water; a lemon twist expressed over top.

Lots of muss and fuss. An effervescent masterpiece. Whisky champagne.

If you're inspired by this approach, try your hand at making the best highball you possibly can.

Use a highball glass (duh) – the more beautiful, the better.

Choose a high quality soda water. Each brand has different levels of carbonation and minerals. You can experiment, but if in doubt, Schweppes is a great option.

Most whiskies work well in a highball. Delicate and fragrant blends are most popular, but don't be limited to them. Soda water amplifies flavors, so any whisky you enjoy generally, you'll enjoy it in a highball.

What ratio of whisky to soda water? 1:3 or 1:4 is most common. For a bolder drink, try 1:2. In Japan, many people drink highballs up to 1:5.

Large, clean, clear ice is best – try carving your own! Fill the glass to the top.

Take care in the preparation; at every step, the goal is to keep the effervescence high and the temperature low.

The method

Chill the glass and whisky in the fridge beforehand.

Pour whisky over ice. Stir.

Pour soda water – not over the ice but down the side, directly into whisky if possible.

To mix, use a long-handled spoon to gently lift the ice then ease it back down.

Spritz a citrus twist over the top for those sweet, sweet oils. Place it on the ice, or down the side.

MIXERS

If anyone's ever given you the impression whisky shouldn't be mixed, it's time to let go of that myth.

Ever since people started drinking whisky, mixing it has been the most popular way to drink it. When you feel like something cold or sweet or bubbly, but you also feel like whisky, mix up a storm, and know that you're part of a proud, centuries-long tradition of whisky mixers.

Mixed drinks are more convenient than a cocktail: 10 seconds, two ingredients, no shaking required. (With fizzy drinks: shaking actively discouraged.) They mellow out the whisky, softening the flavor profile and making the booze more approachable. And whisky makes every other drink better: it infuses them with its rich flavors, completely transforming them into a brand new gustatorial masterpiece.

You don't need my permission to drink whisky with mixers, but I'm giving it to you anyway.

The beauty of the whisky and mixer is its simplicity.

Any glass works. Highball. Lowball. Collins. Coffee mug.

Use plenty of ice . . .

. . . but go easy on the amount of mixer. You can always add more but can't take it back out. My rule of thumb is one-part whisky to two-parts mixer. Find your own sweet spot.

Citrus wedge optional.

MEASURING MATHS

Measuring fizzy mixers in a separate vessel before pouring them into your glass is an express ticket to a flat drink.

The trick is to learn what your favorite glass can hold: fill it with ice, then use a measuring jug of water to see how much liquid fits in. If it's 5 fl oz (150 ml), you know that 1⅔ fl oz (50 ml) of whisky topped off with mixer will give you a ratio of 1:2, while 1 fl oz (30 ml) topped off will be 1:4.

If all this sounds too tedious – just eyeball it. You'll figure out what works.

What whisky?

Many entry-level offerings of the big brands are specifically designed with mixing in mind, with balanced flavor profiles that hold up masterfully with cola or ginger ale. Don't let anybody make you feel bad for turning to a cheaper whisky for a mixed drink.

On the flip side – never let anyone make you feel bad about mixing a nice whisky. Just as a great gin can make an excellent G&T, a great whisky can make an excellent mixed drink. A robust peppery rye. A single malt with a rich fruitcake vibe. Even peated whiskies make a mean mixed drink – wait 'til you hear about the Smoky Cokey.

I say mix whatever you damn well want. I'll share some ideas for complementary flavor pairings below, but don't be afraid to experiment.

What mixers?

The mixer is more than half your drink, so don't skimp to save a few bucks. A high-end mixer with a lower-end whisky can make for a bangin' drink, but a mediocre mixer can make even the best whisky into a flaccid disappointment.

No name cola? Not recommended.

Coca-Cola or Pepsi? Good – and certainly convenient.

Artisanal colas like Fever-Tree, Fentimans, or Karma? Now we're talking!

Cola is a kind of soulmate for whisky. From vanilla to cinnamon to citrus, it contains a world of flavor notes that overlap with whisky's flavors, making for a delicious Venn diagram to inspire your pairings. Bourbon will double down on vanilla and caramel notes. High-rye bourbons bring balance to sweeter colas, while sweeter bourbons will suit artisanal colas with less sugar. An American rye, or a spicy or earthy scotch, will dovetail with cola's spice notes. And the lemon-lime in cola can enhance a citrussy single malt scotch – try Glenfiddich 12 for a softer option, Bruichladdich's Classic Laddie for a complex tie-in, or Arran 10 for a zesty zinger. Your options multiply if you go for a vanilla, cherry, or smoked cola.

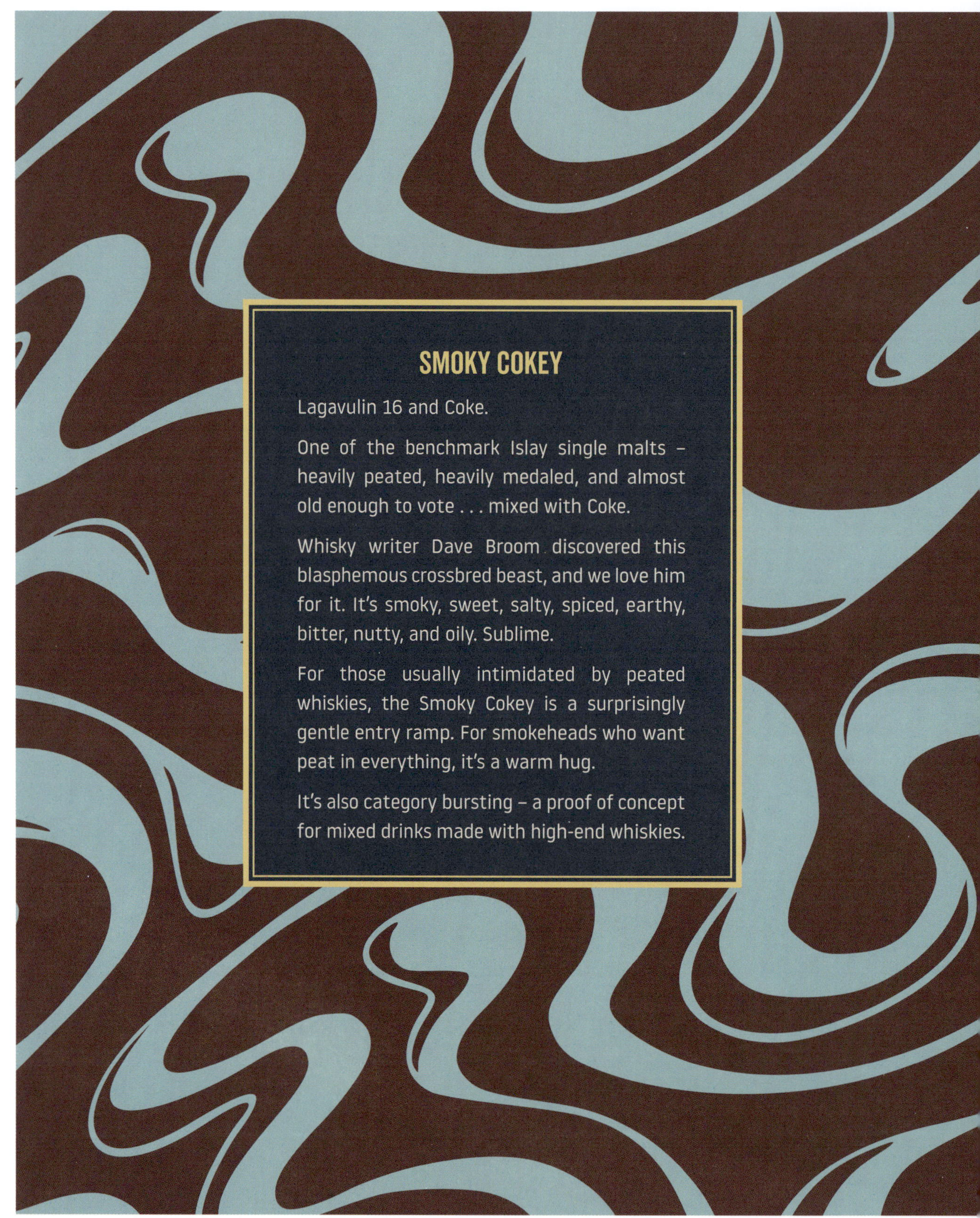

SMOKY COKEY

Lagavulin 16 and Coke.

One of the benchmark Islay single malts – heavily peated, heavily medaled, and almost old enough to vote . . . mixed with Coke.

Whisky writer Dave Broom discovered this blasphemous crossbred beast, and we love him for it. It's smoky, sweet, salty, spiced, earthy, bitter, nutty, and oily. Sublime.

For those usually intimidated by peated whiskies, the Smoky Cokey is a surprisingly gentle entry ramp. For smokeheads who want peat in everything, it's a warm hug.

It's also category bursting – a proof of concept for mixed drinks made with high-end whiskies.

Ginger ale made a name for itself long ago as a versatile mixer for whisky. Easygoing blends – scotch, Canadian, or Irish – melt into its sweet and spicy fizz, while more characterful whiskies add pizzazz. A spice-forward whisky will tie this drink together like nothing else – look for something boasting pepper, baking spices, or even ginger. Create a ginger spice cake in a glass with a whisky featuring notes of candied citrus peel, glacé cherries, walnuts, brown sugar, buttercream, or marmalade. And smoke works superbly with ginger ale – Johnnie Walker Black is an easy win here or choose a peated single malt with idiosyncrasies that appeal to you.

Ginger beer isn't the same as ginger ale, but the same principles mostly apply. Lean into the deeper and darker flavors of scotch; ginger beer can take as much smoke, earthiness, and maritime grit as you can throw at it. Squeeze a wedge of lime in to really sex it up.

Citrus sodas that actually taste like the fruit (like Sanpellegrino) create combos with cocktail-esque vibes. American rye with the fragrant sweetness of orange? That's basically a long, cold old fashioned. Islay scotch with the tangy bitterness of grapefruit? Move over, mezcal – this paloma's gone peaty. Bourbon and the sharp sourness of lemon? Tastes like a whiskey sour in a New York hotel. Or take it to Tokyo with Japanese grain whisky and yuzu soda.

Tonic water with Irish whiskey is called a leprechaun, so obviously you have to drink that at least once – try a sherry-matured blend, or a pot still whiskey that leans toward sweet fruit. A floral or honeyed Highland scotch will melt nicely into a dry tonic. Or take a more direct approach: use a rye or a rye-heavy bourbon with oomph (above 45% ABV) to punch through tonic's bitterness. Some decry whisky and tonic water as blasphemy, but you've read enough of this book to know I don't care.

Tea is a popular pairing with whisky in Asia. For a taste that transports you to a bar in Beijing or a karaoke room in Hong Kong, mix Johnnie Walker Black or Chivas 12 with sweetened bottled green tea. Unsweetened cold brewed green tea allows lighter-flavored whiskies with delicate citrus and floral notes to shine, while roasted teas with smoky flavor profiles are *begging* to interact with smoky whisky.

For some folk in the American South, sweet tea is a fact of life; knock up a pitcher like meemaw used to make, spike it with bourbon, and you'll be happy as a pig in mud.

And who says mixers have to be cold? My friends in Northern Ireland cradle their evening cup of tea like it's the Holy Grail – surely dosing their Cup of Life with the Water of Life would be Bushmills bliss.

Coconut water and whisky may sound bizarre, but in Brazil or Puerto Rico, the locals suck it down – and the tourists are catching on. Coconut water is indescribably refreshing – more hydrating than water itself – as well as silky in the mouth, sweet, and a little bit salty. It's a fine dance partner for whisky; a spicy or smoky blend will samba with that salinity.

The best coconut water is poured fresh from a young green coconut; if you can't get your hands on one of those, find a brand of coconut water with no added sugar, mix to taste then enjoy a drink more refreshing than a piña colada in a pineapple.

Coffee and whisky is called "holiday coffee" at my house.

Fresh apple juice and whiskey will change you. Bourbon, rye, or Irish – any whiskey with an "e." Freshly pressed Granny Smith apples. Cloudy. Foamy. Sweet. Tart. Delicious. Drink immediately.

BOILERMAKERS

Carbs on carbs is always a good idea. Chip sandwiches. Potato pizza. Whisky and beer.

I don't recommend the classic dive bar boilermaker: slam a shot of bottom shelf whisky, chase it with a bland lager to clean your mouth out.

But the modern whisky bar boilermaker is a cut above: sip a quality whisky and a flavorsome beer alongside each other and appreciate both.

Here are some pairing ideas to get the creative juices flowing . . .

- A peppery rye with a bitter Czech pilsner.
- A caramel-forward bourbon with a full-bodied stout.
- A creamy, spicy, fruity Irish pot still with a creamy, spicy, fruity witbier.
- A winey Australian single malt with a rich amber ale.
- A delicate Japanese blend with a fragrant saison.
- A rough-and-ready smoke bomb with a resinous West Coast IPA.

COCKTAILS

Too many people look past whisky when they think of cocktails.

Some think the distinctive flavors of whisky don't play nice with other ingredients. Others say, "Good whisky is wasted in a cocktail!"

But whisky's flavors include fruit and spice, caramel and vanilla . . . these can shine in all kinds of cocktails.

American whiskey is fairly well accepted in the cocktail world because a majority of classic cocktails were American inventions. Rye and bourbon got a head start before Prohibition and then made a strong comeback in cocktails in the 2000s.

Blended scotch is the next most common whisky you'll see in cocktail recipes, but it's a distant third. Other styles trail behind even further.

But no whisky should be disqualified: smooth Irish whiskeys and versatile Canadian blends, fragrant Japanese blends, peated Tasmanian single malts, floral French drops . . . anything's fair game. It's all about finding the right flavor combinations.

There are whisky cocktails for every taste and occasion. A mint julep to cool you down, a hot toddy to warm you up, and an Irish coffee to amp you up. Some highlight the hero ingredient; others create something greater than the sum of its parts.

Personally, I rarely make cocktails exactly as you're "supposed" to. Is it because I'm a wild spirit and a superior breed of human, or because I make do with the random assortment of ingredients in my kitchen and get distracted halfway through a recipe? I'll let you decide.

Thankfully, cocktails are all about experimentation. Begin with the recipes and guidelines that others lay out, but don't feel you need to stay on those highways – take the back roads, go cross country, and see where you end up.

MAKING COCKTAILS

Mixing cocktails is a science – there are rules to learn, formulas to memorize, and experiments to conduct.

It's also an art – creativity, talent, and perseverance will take you far.

Master mixologists have their own language, talking about advanced shaking techniques and obscure European liqueurs you've never heard of. It's enough to make your head spin before you've even taken a sip.

But you know what? Cocktail making is also a game. We do it because making cocktails – and drinking them – is fun.

Use this section as a kicking-off point, but when inspiration strikes, feel free to ignore whichever parts you want.

It's play time.

WHAT EQUIPMENT DO I NEED?

Most kitchens have measuring spoons/cups/jugs, a citrus juicer, a sharp knife, and a vegetable peeler. We've already covered glassware and ice (see "Serving up your whisky"). You don't need a special bar spoon or muddling stick or other fancy gear.

The only "special" items you need to get started are . . .

- a measuring glass (1 fl oz/30 ml or 1⊠ fl oz/50 ml) designed for spirits or espresso
- a cocktail shaker. Go with stainless steel rather than plastic – it won't get stained or absorb smells – plus it looks awesome
- toothpicks.

A FEW KEY INGREDIENTS . . .

Citrus (juice & garnish)

Citrus wheels and twists are common garnishes for whisky cocktails, and freshly squeezed lemon juice is a must for a sour.

If you're going to be juicing the citrus, check first if you need a slice or twist for a garnish; if so, prepare those *before* juicing. It's no fun trying to backpedal on this.

LET'S DO THE TWIST

It takes some practice to master the art of the twist – but it's worth it.

1. Use sharp knife or a vegetable peeler to remove a strip of citrus peel about as long and as wide as your pinky finger.
2. Lay it on the bench with the pith (the white stuff) facing up. Use a knife to scrape off as much of the pith as you reasonably can.
3. Keep the shape of the twist *au naturel* or use a knife to tidy up the edges.
4. Twist or curl the peel above your glass – the essential oils will mist into the air, and you want them to land on your drink.
5. Hang the peel over the edge of the glass or drop it in.

Variations

- Cut the twist as above, roll it up, then pierce through all the layers with a toothpick.
- Cut the peel from a citrus wheel, remove the pith, and wind the peel around a straw or chopstick to make a tight spring.
- A coin-sized circle of peel is simple but striking.

Simple syrup

You'll see simple syrup in a number of cocktail recipes. It's easy to make.

- 8 oz (1 cup) white sugar
- 8 fl oz (1 cup) boiling water

Combine the sugar and water. Stir until dissolved. Cool in the fridge before using. Simple, right?

If a recipe calls for "rich" sugar syrup, up the ratio to 2 parts sugar and bring the mix briefly to the boil in a saucepan to dissolve the sugar.

I've recently learned a cheat's way, too – combine sugar and room temperature water in a blender. Takes a few minutes to properly dissolve the sugar, but it doesn't take hours to cool down. Perfect for a spur-of-the-moment old fashioned.

Store simple syrup in a clean glass container in the fridge; I like to use an old whisky bottle. It should last at least a month.

Aquafaba

Literally means "bean water," but don't let that put you off.

Aquafaba is the liquid strained from a can of chickpeas, and it's an impressive alternative to egg. Many bartenders now use aquafaba as standard for frothing drinks – it has a lovely texture, and a more neutral smell and taste than egg whites. Choose a brand of chickpeas with no added salt.

In cocktails, 1 fl oz (30 ml) aquafaba replaces one egg white or 1½ fl oz (45 ml) replaces a whole egg.

Fat washing

Yes, you read that unappetizing phrase correctly: fat washing.

It means infusing a spirit with a fatty ingredient to impart flavor and give the spirit a silky texture. Think butter, bacon, coconut oil, peanut butter . . . whatever fat you fancy.

Fat-washed whisky is popular as a cocktail ingredient in trendy bars. You can make it at home by mixing a small amount of fat with whisky, placing it in the freezer overnight to separate the fats from the liquid, then straining out the solids. It's best to find a recipe, since each fat behaves differently. You wouldn't want your peanut butter bourbon to turn out *weird*.

OLD FASHIONED

This cocktail's been so trendy in recent years, you'd think it had just been invented. But the old fashioned really is an old cocktail.

The 1800s saw the rise of a drink called the whiskey cocktail – whiskey, sugar, bitters, and citrus peel. When bartenders started getting fancy and adding other liqueurs into the mix, drinkers who didn't want that newfangled stuff would order their whiskey cocktail "the old fashioned way" – and the name stuck.

During Prohibition, people started getting fancy again by adding fruits like orange or pineapple, probably to mask the taste of cheap booze. But a 1944 cocktail book insisted that "serious-minded persons omit fruit salad from 'Old Fashioneds'" and I tend to agree.

In such a minimalist cocktail, every element can level up the experience. So use a whisky you enjoy drinking, because you'll really taste it – bourbon and rye are traditional, but branch out if you feel the urge. Use a big, beautiful ice cube. Use a fat piece of orange peel. Be sure to express the oils over the top of the drink.

But no pineapple, please.

- 1½ fl oz (45 ml) bourbon or rye whiskey
- 1 teaspoon (5 ml) rich sugar syrup (2 parts sugar to 1 part water)
- A few dashes Angostura bitters
- Orange twist

Stir ingredients in a mixing glass with ice, then strain into an old fashioned (rocks) glass with one large fresh ice cube.

Garnish with an orange twist.

You can build it in glass; it's just less tidy.

Serious cocktail aficionados may send a hitman after me for saying this, but: if you feel like a longer drink, add some soda water. It's ah-mazing.

I've used maple syrup in place of sugar, and I've seen someone use a dash of orange liqueur when they didn't have an orange on hand. Is it still an old fashioned? Not really. But it's tasty. Just drink it before the Cocktail Police kick down your door.

FLAMING OIL

Want a bit of theater? Light a match, then squeeze your orange twist to spritz the oils into the flame. Your guests will love seeing the oils flicker and burn in mid-air. And who am I kidding – so will you.

MANHATTAN

"It is but a short time ago that a mixture of whiskey, vermouth, and bitters came into vogue. It went under various names: Manhattan cocktail . . . " – *The Olean Democrat*, September 5, 1882.

There are competing stories about who invented the Manhattan, and precisely where – but we're all agreed on "somewhere on Manhattan Island."

Manhattans are bold, sweet, and velvety. Rye is the classic whiskey to use – and the spice of rye is great for balancing the sweet vermouth – but bourbon's a fine option, too.

- 2 fl oz (60 ml) rye whiskey
- 1 fl oz (30 ml) sweet (red) vermouth
- 1–2 dashes Angostura bitters

Maraschino cherry

Fill a mixing glass with ice and add all ingredients. Stir well.

Strain into a chilled glass – a stemmed glass is more classy; an old fashioned glass is more casual.

Garnish with a maraschino cherry.

Variations

Rob Roy – swap out the American whiskey for blended scotch. (Despite the Scottish folk hero's name and Scottish whisky . . . this too originated in New York.)

Emerald – swap out the American whiskey for Irish. Sláinte.

WHISKEY SOUR

There's a sour cocktail for every spirit, but whiskey sours are the most popular (because they're the best, obviously). They're sweet and sour and strong – it's just about getting the balance right.

Everyone's got their own opinion on the perfect proportions, so play around to find yours. My ratio makes a more bourbon-forward sour; I get annoyed if I suspect the sourness or sweetness is getting in the way of my whiskey.

- 2 fl oz (60 ml) bourbon
- ⅔ fl oz (20 ml) fresh squeezed lemon juice
- ⅔ fl oz (20 ml) sugar syrup
- ⅔ fl oz (20 ml) aquafaba or egg white
- A few dashes of Angostura bitters
- Maraschino cherry

Add the first four ingredients to a cocktail shaker. Dry shake (shake without ice) to froth the drink, then add ice and shake until cold. Strain into a chilled glass.

Stain the foam with a few dashes of Angostura bitters and garnish with a maraschino cherry.

Some leave out the aquafaba/egg white (and so skip the dry shaking step), but I never do – it ties the flavors together perfectly, adds a smooth texture, and the white froth on top looks gorgeous.

Variations

New York sour – seems like it shouldn't work, but it definitely does. Pour ½ fl oz (15 ml) of shiraz or malbec gently over the back of a spoon to float it on top of the sour. Don't bother with a garnish – the red layer of wine is striking enough.

Canadian Maple Leaf – the original Maple Leaf simply swaps out the sugar syrup for maple syrup and the cherry for a lemon twist, but I say go extra Canadian and swap out the bourbon for Canadian whisky as well. Makes sense, eh?

HOT TODDY

We're all wondering the same thing: why's it called a "toddy"?

The English will tell you it's a bastardization of "taddy," a drink that arose in 17th century British India.

The Irish will tell you a doctor named Robert Bentley Todd prescribed a mixture of hot water, brandy, sugar, and cinnamon to his patients.

The Scottish will say the toddy harks back to when pubs in Edinburgh would mix whisky with hot water, and that water was from Tod's Well.

Are all three true? Are any of them? Don't ask me. But people still turn to toddies when they have a cold, so I reckon we give 10 points to Ireland.

Having said that, a big oily scotch makes for an excellent hot toddy . . .

- 2 oz (60 ml) whisky
- ½ fl oz / 3 teaspoons (15 ml) honey
- Juice of half a small lemon (slice up the rest)
- Cinnamon stick (and any other spices – cloves, star anise)
- Hot water
- Warm a mug or heatproof glass with boiling water (then tip it out).

Combine the whiskey, honey, and lemon juice in the warmed mug. Top up with boiling water and stir until the honey is dissolved.

Garnish with a cinnamon stick and a couple of lemon slices.

Some people also add star anise or cloves. I'm not a huge fan of either, but clove-studded lemon sure does look cool.

PENICILLIN

A penicillin cocktail's kind of halfway between a whisky sour and a hot toddy. Plus ginger. Plus peat.

It was invented in 2005 by an Aussie bartender (Sam Ross) in a New York bar (Milk & Honey) using Scottish whisky (blended + Lagavulin 16). What a killer combo!

Will the medicinal effect of honey and lemon be enough to replace antibiotics? Probably not. But did this cocktail change the world as much as the discovery of penicillin? . . . Also probably not.

It is very popular, though. You could say it's . . . infectious. (Wait – that's the opposite of penicillin.)

- 2 fl oz (60 ml) blended scotch
- ¾ fl oz (22.5 ml) fresh squeezed lemon juice
- ¾ fl oz (22.5 ml) honey ginger syrup
- ¼ fl oz (7.5 ml) peated Islay scotch
- Candied ginger

Fill a cocktail shaker with ice and add the first three ingredients. Shake until cold.

Fill an old fashioned glass filled with ice, then strain the drink into it.

Float the Islay scotch on top of the drink by gently pouring it over the back of a spoon.

Garnish with a piece of candied ginger on a skewer.

Honey ginger syrup

- *1 cup honey*
- *1 cup water*
- *3 ½ oz (100 g) fresh ginger, peeled, and finely sliced*

Combine the ingredients in a saucepan. Bring to a boil then simmer over reduced heat for 5 minutes. Steep in the fridge for 12 hours, then strain into a jar with a lid. It'll be good for 3 days.

IRISH COFFEE

The year's 1943, and it's a stormy winter's night. In County Limerick, Ireland, a recently departed plane is forced to return to Foynes Airport. To warm up the cold and weary passengers, chef Joe Sheridan makes a round of black coffees with whipped cream on top – and some sneaky whiskey in there, too.

A passenger asked, "Are these Brazilian coffees?" to which Joe quips, "No – they're Irish coffees!"

That's the legend, anyway.

When choosing your whiskey, Tullamore D.E.W. is a traditional option, but you can always use something bolder or fancier. It's hard to mess this up.

- 4–6 fl oz (120–175 ml) freshly brewed black coffee
- 1⅓ fl oz (40 ml) Irish whiskey
- 2 teaspoons sugar (I suggest brown sugar)
- Chilled heavy cream

Warm a glass goblet with boiling water (then tip it out). Pour in coffee until the glass is three-quarters full, stir in the sugar until it dissolves, then stir in the whiskey.

Whip the cream lightly. One way is to shake it in a chilled cocktail shaker until thickened; your guests will be thrilled. Float the cream on top by pouring gently over the back of a spoon.

You can use more whiskey. You can use less sugar. About the only thing you shouldn't do is ruin the layers by mixing the cream in.

BLACK SHIP

For over 200 years, Japan was a closed country . . . until 1853, when Commodore Matthew Perry (not the guy from F.R.I.E.N.D.S.) sailed four warships into Port Edo, demanding that Japan open its doors to the US for trade. Rude.

At least he brought a gift – several barrels of American whiskey for the Emperor.

That was the end of Japan's period of seclusion, and the beginning of its love affair with the golden spirit.

Fast forward to now, and Japan sends its own whisky around the world. This rich, fruity cocktail showcases the excellence of Japanese whisky – which is more subtle than those first Black Ships.

- 1½ fl oz (45 ml) Japanese whisky
- 1 fl oz (30 ml) pomegranate juice
- ¼ fl oz (7.5 ml) port
- 1 teaspoon (5 ml) freshly squeezed lemon juice

Fill a cocktail shaker with ice and add all ingredients.

Shake well for 15 seconds.

Strain through a fine mesh strainer into a chilled martini glass.

Garnish with a lemon twist.

Talk about a blast of flavor. (That's a cannon joke . . . did I mention those ships were loaded with cannons?)

COFFEE AND CIGARETTES

This cocktail's a brainchild of Thomas Waugh, giant of the New York bartending scene and former barista. If you're keen to recreate the original recipe, it calls for Caol Ila 12 year, Galliano Ristretto, Carpano Antica Formula vermouth, and Bittermen's Xocolatl Mole bitters.

Personally, I'm happy to go off brand and call it "experimentation." As long as the Islay scotch is smoky, the coffee liqueur is punchy, the vermouth is sweet, and the bitters are chocolatey, you'll do okay.

- 2 fl oz (60 ml) peated Islay scotch
- ½ fl oz (15 ml) coffee liqueur
- 1 teaspoon (5 ml) sweet (red) vermouth
- 2 dashes chocolate bitters

Fill a mixing glass with ice and add all ingredients.

Stir for at least 30 seconds, then strain into a chilled Nick & Nora glass.

No garnish. Who garnishes their coffee and cigarettes?

BREAKFAST IN THE WEST

I invented this cocktail, and in my humble opinion . . . it's the friggin' best.

Bourbon and orange go *brilliantly* together. You can't argue with that; it's a law of nature. The day I learned that law, I was immediately inspired to create my own bourbon and orange cocktail.

I wanted something strong, but not too short. It had to be very simple, for when I can't be bothered. It had to be well balanced because I didn't want a sweet mess.

After a little tinkering, I landed on this drink. I call it "breakfast in the west", because I figure if you're a cowboy, bourbon can count as breakfast as long as it has orange in it.

- 1 fl oz (30 ml) bourbon (chilled)
- 1 fl oz (30 ml) Cointreau (chilled)
- 2 fl oz (60 ml) soda water
- Orange twist

Pour chilled bourbon, Cointreau, and soda water into an old fashioned glass.

Garnish with an orange twist.

That's it. As my skeptical friends have all discovered, it tastes far better than such a simple drink has any right to be.

Oh, and if you feel like a longer drink? Add more soda water. Now it's a long breakfast in the west.

RUSTY NAIL

Don't let the name fool you – there's nothing rough about a rusty nail.

Sweet and spicy and smooth as Sinatra, this two-ingredient classic was a favorite of Ol' Blue Eyes himself. The honeyed liqueur takes the edge off the whisky's bite, and adds a resonant croon of its own.

Simple. Timeless. Won't give you tetanus.

- 1½ fl oz (45 ml) blended scotch
- ¾ fl oz (22.5 ml) Drambuie
- Lemon twist

Pour both ingredients over plenty of ice in an old fashioned (rocks) glass.

Stir gently.

Garnish with a lemon twist.

MINT JULEP

The official drink of the Kentucky Derby, this dangerously refreshing "smash" hits the spot faster than Secretariat crossing the finish line in the final race of the 1973 Triple Crown. Mint juleps are traditionally served in a metal cup (if you can be bothered to find one) with a mountain of ice to make it frostier than Elsa's palace.

And be gentle when you muddle the mint leaves – you want to bruise them, not puree them.

- 2 fl oz (60 ml) bourbon
- ¼ fl oz (7.5 ml) simple syrup
- 8 mint leaves
- Mint sprig, to garnish

Muddle the mint leaves with the simple syrup in a highball or metal julep cup.

Overfill the glass with cracked ice, so it's heaped above the rim.

Add the bourbon and stir until the outside of the glass is frosted.

Garnish with a mint sprig.

Be sure to sip your julep right near the mint sprig for a faceful of minty freshness.

BOULEVARDIER

This drink about town is often described as a whisky negroni, and you can get cocktail nerds arguing by asking, “Which came first – the negroni or the boulevardier?”

Oh, and in case you were wondering: it’s pronounced bool-a-var-dee-ay.

(If anyone should know how to pronounce an American whiskey cocktail with a French name, it’s an Australian writer with a German surname.)

- 1½ fl oz (45 ml) bourbon
- 1 fl oz (30 ml) Campari
- 1 fl oz (30 ml) sweet (red) vermouth
- Orange twist

Pour all ingredients over plenty of ice in a chilled rocks glass. Stir gently to mix.

Alternatively, stir with ice in a shaker, then strain into your glass of choice.

Garnish with an orange twist.

ITALIAN GENTLEMAN

If a whiskey sour and a boulevardier had a baby, it would taste like this. Bitter, sweet, sour, strong, charming, vivacious . . . this modern signore has it all.

- 1½ fl oz (45 ml) bourbon
- 1½ fl oz (45 ml) Campari
- ¾ fl oz (22.5 ml) freshly squeezed lemon juice
- ¼ fl oz (7.5 ml) simple syrup
- A dash of orange bitters

Add everything to a cocktail shaker and shake with ice for 20 seconds, then strain into a chilled coupe glass.

SAZERAC

This is an old fashioned that's been to New Orleans. The Sazerac starts out simple – rye, sugar, bitters – but then takes a jazzy turn with a drizzle of absinthe that transforms the whole drink.

Like the best jazz musicians, feel free to improvise if the mood takes you. Sub out absinthe for another anise liqueur. Sub out Peychaud's bitters for another bitters. You'll anger the Sazerac purists, but you'll still make a boppin' drink.

- 1½ fl oz (45 ml) rye whiskey
- 1 teaspoon (5 ml) rich sugar syrup (2 parts sugar to 1 part water)
- 3 dashes Peychaud's bitters
- ¼ fl oz (7.5 ml) absinthe or anise liqueur
- Lemon twist

Fill an old fashioned (rocks) glass with ice, and set it aside.

Pour the rye, rich sugar syrup and bitters into a mixing glass. Fill with ice and stir well.

Discard the ice from the first glass. Pour in the absinthe, swirl it around to coat the glass, then discard the excess or tip it into a shot glass.

Strain the cocktail into the absinthe-coated old fashioned glass.

Express the oils from the lemon twist over the drink, but don't drop the peel in; balance it on the edge or throw it away.

Some people drink the excess absinthe alongside the Sazerac. Others tip it down the sink. Follow your heart.

TIPPERARY

If you're anything like me, the mere mention of this drink is enough to get "It's a Long Way to Tipperary" stuck in your head for the next three days. And it's not just the name that's memorable; the bittersweet, herbal taste will stick with you, too.

My recipe uses slightly more whiskey than most, but I like to think any Irish soldier would approve of my generous pour.

One sip of this WWI era cocktail and you'll be longing for home – assuming your hometown is in the middle of Ireland.

- 1¾ fl oz (52.5 ml) Irish whiskey
- 1 fl oz (30 ml) sweet (red) vermouth
- ½ fl oz (15 ml) green Chartreuse
- 2 dashes Angostura bitters
- Orange twist

Add all ingredients to a mixing glass with ice. Stir until chilled.

Strain into a Nick & Nora glass.

Garnish with an orange twist.

WHISKY MAC

Forget the idea that Scots are angry; this is one of the most forgiving drinks you'll ever . encounter.

With ice? Without ice? With boiling water to turn it into a toddy? The whisky Mac doesn't mind. It has one job: to warm you from the inside out.

- 1½ fl oz (45 ml) blended scotch
- 1 fl oz (30 ml) ginger wine

Fill an old fashioned (rocks) glass with ice – if you want.

Add the scotch and ginger wine.

Stir to combine – or don't.

Blended scotch and ginger wine. Forget all else, you'll still be fine.

SCOTCH ESPRESSO MARTINI

I don't care if I sound like a boring old man: standard espresso martinis are too sweet for my liking. But swap out the vodka for scotch, and suddenly it just *works.*

And if it's peaty scotch? Sssssmokin'! Somebody stop me!

(Hi, I just woke up from a 30-year coma. Is it still funny to quote Jim Carrey movies?)

- 1½ fl oz (45 ml) scotch
- 1 fl oz (30 ml) coffee liqueur
- 1 fl oz (30 ml) freshly brewed espresso (or other strong coffee), cooled
- Coffee beans

Fill a cocktail shaker with ice and add all ingredients.

Shake vigorously until well-chilled and frothy.

Strain into a chilled martini glass.

Garnish with three coffee beans placed gently on the foam.

If you have a sweet tooth, add a little simple syrup to taste.

You can use Irish whiskey if you prefer. Or rye. If I'm being honest, pretty much any whisky makes a bangin' espresso martini.

TORONTO

This rye-forward cocktail walks the line between a Manhattan and an old fashioned, with a bittersweet punch from Fernet-Branca (a kind of amaro).

Did it originate in Toronto? Who knows. Does the Fernet make it medicinal? Absolutely not. Is it worth drinking? Yeah, no, definitely.

- 2 fl oz (60 ml) Canadian rye whisky
- 1/4 fl oz (7.5 ml) Fernet-Branca
- 1/4 fl oz (7.5 ml) simple syrup
- 2 dashes Angostura bitters
- Orange twist

Stir ingredients in a mixing glass with ice, then strain into an old fashioned (rocks) glass with one large fresh ice cube.

Garnish with an orange twist.

If you want to really Canadian this drink up, swap out the simple syrup for maple syrup, eh?

BLOOD AND SAND

Whisky's the color of sand (sort of). Sweet vermouth and Heering cherry liqueur look like blood (sort of). Orange juice . . . well, that's a strange choice.

This cocktail may be an unlikely concoction, but it's managed to stick around for a hundred years. Some love it. Some hate it. Find where you stand with a blood and sand.

- ¾ fl oz (22.5 ml) blended scotch
- ¾ fl oz (22.5 ml) Heering cherry liqueur
- ¾ fl oz (22.5 ml) sweet (red) vermouth
- ¾ fl oz (22.5 ml) freshly squeezed orange juice
- Orange twist

Fill a cocktail shaker with ice and add all ingredients.

Shake well for 15 seconds.

Strain through a fine mesh strainer into a chilled coupe glass.

Garnish with an orange twist.

TOKYO SIDECAR

Any time I find myself with a bottle of brandy in the cupboard (usually after Christmas), I end up drinking sidecars. But you know what's better than a classic sidecar made with leftover cheap brandy? A Tokyo sidecar made with silky Japanese whisky and tangy yuzu.

- 2 fl oz (60 ml) Japanese whisky
- ¾ fl oz (22.5 ml) Cointreau
- ½ fl oz (15 ml) yuzu juice
- Yuzu peel

Fill a cocktail shaker with ice and add all ingredients.

Shake well for 15 seconds.

Strain into a chilled martini glass.

Garnish with a twist of yuzu.

In a pinch, you can use lemon instead of yuzu.

PICKLEBACK

I feel like the invention of the pickleback was a cruel practical joke that got out of hand and became a global phenomenon. Many people say it's surprisingly good. I say it's gustatory self-flagellation for people who want to punish their tastebuds.

- A shot of Irish whiskey (What a waste.)
- A shot of pickle juice (Why?)

Shoot the whiskey. (Please don't.)

Shoot the pickle juice. (I'm begging you. Just stop.)

Question your life choices. (I warned you.)

MAKING MEMORIES WITH WHISKY

Whisky inspires songs. It symbolizes sophistication. It can transport you to another country, or even another century. It can make you feel like a different person, and like the best version of yourself.

I've said you should drink whisky however you enjoy it, and I mean that. Work your way through a cocktail book. Mix it with cola as you watch the football. Add three drops of water and sniff it thoughtfully in the corner of a speakeasy.

But if you only ever drink it one way, you're missing a lot of what whisky has to offer. To get philosophical: you're also missing a lot of what *life* has to offer. When you fill your life with new and different experiences, your brain perceives time differently so that the days, the weeks, the years feel like they last for longer. Time doesn't fly; it slows down. You actually get more life.

What could be more appropriate to give you those life-giving experiences than the water of life itself?

SUNNY DAY

The bracing freshness of a whiskey sour is as good as a cool breeze on a hot day. Or if you can't be bothered making cocktails when it's so beautiful outside, keep it simple with mixers. Spike a jug of sweet iced tea with bourbon and show your friends some southern hospitality, or capture the Great White North by splashing Canadian whisky over ice and topping up with ginger ale. Mix blended scotch with coconut water and a squeeze of lime to go on a Caribbean holiday, or with iced green tea to enjoy a humid summer's day in Hong Kong.

COLD NIGHT

When we first got together, my wife and I loved to drive up to a mountainside lookout on a cool winter's evening. We'd talk for hours, watching the city lights and sipping boozy hot chocolates. Twenty years later, a thermos of hot chocolate and a hip flask of whisky still makes us feel like teenagers.

For a more mature option, listen to 1800s booze writer Charles Tovey: "Many a noble man will leave the choicest wine to indulge in his glass of toddy." So end your dinner party by retiring to the parlor with a round of hot toddies for your guests. Even if they're not Victorian English nobility, it'll warm their hands and their hearts.

THE REALLY SPECIAL BOTTLE

When my friends chipped in and bought me that bottle of 25-year-old Glenfarclas for my 25th birthday, I think I kissed them. But as keen as I was to drink it, I made myself a rule: I would only drink it with other people – never on my own.

It was a great decision. I was always excited to share that whisky with friends who'd enjoy it, and there was a sense of occasion every time I brought it out.

Next time you get a special bottle of whisky – whether it's a gift, a splurge, or a souvenir from your travels – consider putting my rule in place. It may seem strange to limit your own access to your own whisky, but it gives a bottle a magical glow. And while you'll actually drink *less* of it yourself, you'll enjoy it *more* than if you drank it on your own.

OLD FASHIONED STATION

If you invite people over to your house and offer them an old fashioned, they'll think you're cool. If you set up a station where your guests can make their own old fashioned, they'll *know* you're cool.

It's fairly simple, as long as you triple check that you have all the ingredients and equipment you'll need. I recommend making yourself an old fashioned the day before the event and noting every single thing you use, including the cutting board where you prepare your twist and the cloth you use when you shoot bitters onto the bench. Decide whether you'll put out a small cooler of ice cubes or keep them in an easy-to-access part of the freezer.

You can go classic with a mid-range bourbon or rye, or lean left of center with an interesting single malt or cask strength rye. You can put out multiple whiskies, so people can choose the one that appeals most to them. You can even encourage them to taste and compare different old fashioneds throughout the evening.

Write out an instruction card in advance and demonstrate how to make an old fashioned when your guests arrive. If someone seems underconfident, let them know you're happy to make their drinks if they'd prefer – you are the host, after all.

It's a bit of work. But your guests will love it.

THE HEIGHT OF SOPHISTICATION

I know, I know, I've said whisky isn't only for sipping neat from a crystal tumbler and being all suave and sophisticated . . .

. . . but sometimes it is.

Dress up in your finest outfit and go to a whisky bar where the bartenders wear waistcoats and climb a wooden ladder to get to the rare bottles. Sit back on a Chesterfield sofa and swirl the liquid gold in your glass. Close your eyes and breathe in the spice and oak and leather while a jazz trio fills the air with the silver sounds of moonlight.

I love tapping into that old world charm from time to time. It makes me feel like one of the richest people in the world.

WATCHING FILMS AND TV

The Maltese Falcon (1941) – Come on, Sam Spade – you should know better than to accept a drink from the villain. Luckily, we know from the book that the hardboiled detective keeps a bottle of Manhattan cocktail in his desk drawer. Perhaps that's the safer option here.

The Godfather Part I and Part II (1972 & 1974) – Godfather movies, Godfather cocktail. For Part I, use the original proportions of equal parts blended scotch and amaretto – it's good, but intense. For Part II, dial down the amaretto to a 4:1 or even 8:1 ratio – it's more nuanced and interesting. If you watch Part III, just drink amaretto – it's a little bitter.

Highlander (1985) – How do you improve a movie about immortal sword fighters who chase each other from the Scottish Highlands to New York, where one will prevail and become a powerful telepath? With a double Glenmorangie.

Lost In Translation (2003) – This film helped to fuel the popularity of Japanese whisky around the world. Drink a Hibiki, chuckle at Bill Murray's deadpan expressions, and pity his poor jet-lagged character who complains about starring in a whisky ad for two million dollars. (Suntory, if you're reading this: I will gladly wear a tuxedo and do bad Roger Moore impressions for two million dollars.)

Mad Men (2007–2015) – While the ad men drink plenty of whiskey on its own, most of the brands that show up are entry-level drops by today's standards. Stick with the old fashioneds if you want to feel classy.

Parks and Recreation (2009–2015) – Your only option here is Ron Swanson's nectar of the gods – Lagavulin. Seven seasons, seven bottles. Don't argue.

John Wick (2014) – Enjoy Blanton's Single Barrel on the rocks while Keanu shoots his way through hordes of bad guys. Please don't make a game of drinking each time he kills someone – you won't survive the film.

JAMES BOND

James Bond has a special place in my heart, and whisky has a special place in his. In Ian Fleming's books, Bond drinks far more whisky than martinis. Unfortunately, the movies tone down Bond's love of whisky, but there's still enough to inspire a 007 movie marathon with pairings . . .

Goldfinger (1964) – Enjoy a mint julep alongside Bond and our titular villain.

You Only Live Twice (1967) – We see Bond with Suntory Old Whisky, but nowadays I expect he'd be on a Yamazaki or Hakushu highball.

On Her Majesty's Secret Service (1969) – Sip a single malt scotch with water. Bonus points if you wear a flamboyant lace ruffle around your neck. Oh, behave!

Live And Let Die (1973) – Drink a Sazerac if you have a sense of adventure and want a taste of New Orleans. Drink a bourbon with no ice if you want to get abducted via a secret rotating wall or sinking trapdoor.

The Living Daylights (1987) – The name's Beam. Jim Beam.

GoldenEye (1995) – I wouldn't usually drink Jack Daniel's on the rocks, but when M offers you a drink, you say yes.

The World Is Not Enough (1999) & Die Another Day (2002) – Talisker. M's taste has evolved.

Skyfall (2012) & Spectre (2015) – Daniel Craig's Bond favors Macallan. If you get the 1962 Fine and Rare, don't pour it into a shot glass. It's a waste of good scotch.

No Time To Die (2021) – See James off into the great black beyond with Johnnie Walker Black Label. Since he drinks it in Jamaica, mix it with ginger beer or coconut water.

HOLIDAY COFFEE

For at least a decade, it's been a tradition in our household whenever we have time off work: splash some whisky into your black coffee, breathe in the rising steam and take a glorious sip, and you're officially on holidays.

It's a simple pleasure, inspired by cowboys pouring bourbon in their brew for extra warmth as they camped out on the prairie. But when you consider all that goes into it – the coffee beans grown on another continent, the oak cut and crafted into barrels, the artfully made spirit aged for years before bottling – you realize it's the stuff of kings.

A blended scotch or Canadian works well, or an easygoing bourbon. But a fruity or floral Japanese blend paired with single origin Ethiopian beans is pretty damn good, too.

When you're pouring the whisky, start small. You can always add more, but trying to take it back out is a little harder. I splash in maybe a third of a shot, maybe less. It doesn't sound like much, but it's enough to infuse the coffee with a quiet fire – not an inferno, but a candle.

(Meanwhile, James Bond drinks a 3:1 mix of bourbon to coffee. Yikes.)

Happy holidays!

CHRISTMAS

Forget rum balls made with cheap rum. Peated scotch balls will blow your little mind. A friend of mine made a batch using 50 bucks' worth of Caol Ila. Cost effective? Not at all. Delicious? Definitely.

And who says Santa has to eat cookies and milk? When my wife and I finally finish wrapping presents at 11pm on Christmas Eve, we eat dense Christmas cake with a wedge of flavorsome cheese and a glass of whisky.

Sounds like a strange pairing, but we were inspired by a James Herriot story. The vet gets an emergency callout on Christmas morning and the grateful farmer invites James inside for Christmas cake, Wensleydale cheese, and whisky. James discovers that it's an exquisite combination – and so did we.

Of course, if you're making your own Christmas cake or pudding, I don't need to tell you what to do . . .

I'll tell you anyway – put whisky in it.

ROMANTIC DATE

A picnic rug beside the river at sunset. A packet of fancy potato chips or roasted nuts. The mixings for a whisky cocktail, including a container of ice and two crystal glasses unwrapped from a tea towel.

Unforgettable.

In a pinch, you could simplify this by pre-mixing your cocktail at home and using plastic cups . . . but it doesn't have the same impact. Show your date they're worth the effort.

MAKING WHISKY AND FOOD WORK TOGETHER

If someone tells you whisky doesn't go with food, you have my permission to block your ears and say "LA-LA-LA-LA." You don't need that kind of negativity in your life.

Sure, it can be difficult to match *neat* whisky with food, since the alcohol slams your tastebuds and makes it hard to pick up subtle flavors. But remember: neat is only one of the ways to drink whisky.

So ignore the naysayers. Ignore the experts with their "rules" of whisky and food. They're good at what they do . . . but they're not here right now.

TOASTED SANDWICHES

They go by many names – toasted sandwiches, grilled cheese, jaffles – but whatever you call them, toasties are the stuff of life. On their own, they're delicious. Washed down with whisky, they're absolutely bangin'.

The aim is to cut through the hot, greasy, salty goodness. A whiskey sour can do the trick, but I'm partial to a highball, or even better, a long breakfast in the west. Cold. Carbonated. Kickass.

I'm a big fan of taking toasties to the next level. I like fat slices of sourdough bread, two types of cheese, maybe some tomato, salt flakes, red onion, and a blob of mustard pickle or caramelized onion relish.

A Friday night in front of your favorite sitcom with a couple of fancy toasties (one is never enough) and lazily poured highballs . . . that's what happiness tastes like.

PANCAKES

A day that starts with pancakes is always a good day. A day that starts with whisky pancakes is even better.

They're stupidly easy to make. Start with any pancake recipe and just replace some of the liquid with whisky (about four tablespoons per cup of flour). I like the vanilla and caramel flavors that bourbon brings, but any whisky can work – play around with others to add subtle fruity, spicy, or smoky notes.

The pancakes themselves won't be boozy, since most of the alcohol cooks off. But the bourbon-spiked maple syrup you pour over them? Strong flavor, strong warmth, strong start to the day.

DESSERT

I cannot think of a single dessert that wouldn't be improved with whisky.

Brownies? Bourbon brownies.

Apple strudel? Apple strudel with whisky-soaked raisins.

Banoffee pie? Banoffeeisky pie.

Tiramisu? Well, still tiramisu – but the biscuits are soaked in coffee and whisky.

Find a caramel sauce recipe and add whisky until it's so good you're annoyed you have to share it. You can drizzle it over ice cream, dip fruit in it . . . heck, you can drink it if you want. No jury in the world would convict you.

(Seriously, none. It's not even close to being a crime.)

CHOCOLATES AND NIBBLES

Chocolate and whisky are a versatile duo. I could say lighter whiskies cut through creamy milk chocolate, and sweeter whiskies balance the bitterness of dark chocolate . . . but honestly, it's hard to stuff it up.

Drink Octomore with chocolate truffles and you won't care if the world burns down around you. You might not even notice.

Salted cashews will boost a bright, fruity whisky.

Dried fruit stands up to the potent flavors of peat.

Smoked almonds and breakfast in the west. Trust me.

In summary: whisky is good; snacks are good; whisky and snacks are good.

JAPANESE

In Japan, food and drink are treated with precision and subtlety . . . but I've never been there, and no one's ever accused me of being precise. Or subtle. So my pairings of whisky and Japanese cuisine won't give you an authentic cultural experience. But they will give you cravings for sushi.

Vegetable tempura calls for a well-poured Japanese highball. A whisky with fruity notes (like a Tenjaku blend or Nikka From The Barrel) will elevate the fresh seasonal vegetables, while the lively bubbles will cut through the crunchy batter like a katana through . . . well, pretty much anything.

The soft sweetness of inari gives a blank canvas for other delicate flavors to shine. This is a perfect opportunity to try whisky that uses Mizunara casks and experience the unique notes of Japanese oak – try Shinobu, or a Yamazaki single malt.

Drink pairings with sushi always focus on subtlety. Look for labels promising lighter flavors: apple, pear, melon, florals, cherry blossoms coated with a dusting of late winter snow . . .

But if you're going heavy on pickled ginger and wasabi, skip the subtle approach. Mix up a black ship cocktail to fight fire with fire, or lean into the seaweed flavor with a briny Oban or Old Pulteney.

JAM AND MARMALADE

I may sound like an illustrated bear, but: I absolutely love marmalade, especially when it's homemade. And more again when whisky's in the mix.

I know what some of you are thinking: "But making jam takes ages!"

You know what else takes ages to make? Whisky. So shut up, slip on your apron, and start peeling fruit.

For strawberry jam, choose a whisky with flavors that won't get lost in the sticky sweetness – vanilla, chocolate, or even herbal notes work well.

Orange marmalade goes from awesome to orgasmic with a dose of spicy rye, or a single malt with dried fruit notes. Add Angostura bitters – now it's an old fashioned marmalade.

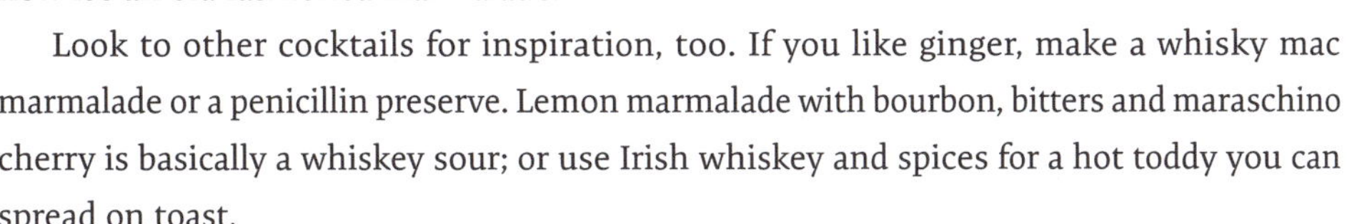

Look to other cocktails for inspiration, too. If you like ginger, make a whisky mac marmalade or a penicillin preserve. Lemon marmalade with bourbon, bitters and maraschino cherry is basically a whiskey sour; or use Irish whiskey and spices for a hot toddy you can spread on toast.

Bonus tip: whisky marmalade makes a mean glaze for kebabs. You're welcome.

SAUCE

Bourbon BBQ sauce is the bomb. It's all about the layers of flavor: bourbon and brown sugar bring the sweetness, vinegar brings the acidity, a little hot sauce brings the heat, and a dash of liquid smoke brings the badassery. Slather it straight onto your burger, or use it as a marinade to supercharge your barbecue. There'll also be plenty of bourbon left for drinking while you're cooking. And eating. And lying on the couch after eating too much.

Sweet and spicy Asian sauces are also perfect for spiking with whisky. Kung pao sauce already has kick, but when you add whisky it uses both feet. Stir in the whisky right before serving for maximum vibrancy; something with citrus notes will find harmony with the Sichuan spice, but any sweet fruit or nutty notes will tie in well. And don't ignore the other elements: coat the chicken or tofu in cornflour before cooking to get that crispy texture, and make sure your wok is scary hot before adding the veggies and spice ingredients to get that smoky char.

CAKE

For one of my birthdays, my wife made me an orange bundt cake drizzled with Cointreau and bourbon syrup, and sprinkled with shards of smoked almond toffee. Stuck in the hole in the middle of the cake? A lowball tumbler containing a breakfast in the west. She is the actual best.

Another year, it was Guinness chocolate cake with Irish whiskey ganache. Strongly recommend. But please don't decorate it with gimmicky little clovers.

WHISKY INFUSIONS

Blood orange bourbon? Hazelnut Irish whiskey? Peated scotch with cacao nibs? Drooling yet?

You can infuse whisky with fruit, or nuts, or spices . . . or anything, really. Put your ingredient into a small jar or bottle, pour in the whisky, then seal it, and let it steep. It should take less than a week but be sure to taste it each day. Want more flavor? Shake it up and check it again tomorrow. Happy with how it tastes? Strain it and enjoy.

These make excellent gifts. Give someone a little bottle of hazelnut Irish whiskey and they'll love you forever.

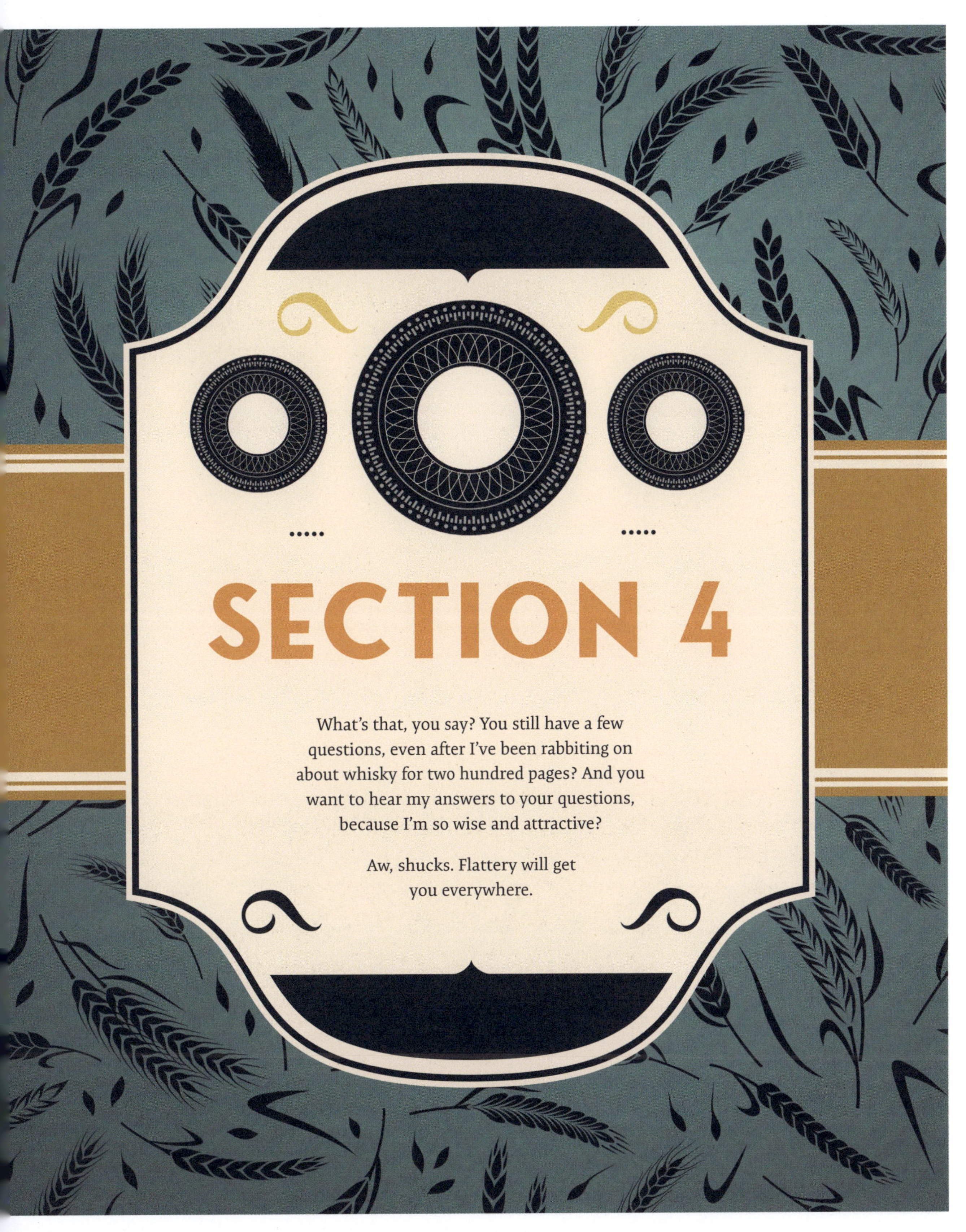

SECTION 4

What's that, you say? You still have a few questions, even after I've been rabbiting on about whisky for two hundred pages? And you want to hear my answers to your questions, because I'm so wise and attractive?

Aw, shucks. Flattery will get you everywhere.

ASK MICK

I'M NEW TO WHISKY, AND I KIND OF THINK IT ALL TASTES THE SAME. WHERE DO I START?

There are a couple of ways you can approach this – what I call 'the familiar approach' and 'the fire approach.'

The familiar approach: Start with flavors you already know and enjoy, and invite whisky to join them. Over time, this will expand your idea of what whisky is and what it can taste like – and you'll enjoy every part of the journey.

If you like the sweet kiss and bitter bite of a negroni, a boulevardier will offer something a little darker and smoother. Use bourbon to emphasize the sweetness, or rye to introduce some spice.

If you like sour things, well, a whiskey sour cocktail is a classic for a reason.

If espresso martinis are your jam, try switching it up with a scotch espresso martini.

Mixing cola with a smoky scotch is a way to dip your toe into peat flavors.

Coffee and hot chocolate are both improved tenfold with a dash of whisky.

I'm yet to meet someone who doesn't like whiskey and apple.

A highball is the ideal way to come face to face with the flavors in a whisky without the burn of sipping it neat. It's like diving in a shark cage – you get to see the majestic creature up close, but with no risk to life and limb.

The fire approach: You want to acquire a taste for neat whisky. You want to develop your palate. You have a vision of yourself in the future, sitting in front of a fire sipping whisky from a crystal glass. And you're willing to walk through the flames to get there.

Start by comparing whiskies with obvious differences. A Glenfiddich and a Lagavulin. A gentle bourbon and a peppery rye. A 40% ABV and a cask strength.

Then move on to comparing similar whiskies. Pick two of the same style, or even from the same distillery, and try to articulate the differences between them. Which is more aromatic? Which is sweeter? Which has more vanilla or caramel or fruit or spice?

Whisky bars are your friend. Choose a time when the bar isn't busy and ask the bartender for recommendations – along with any other questions you have.

Don't be afraid to add water. It reduces alcohol burn and makes it easier to pick up flavors.

Take notes. The more you engage your mind, the better you get at tasting. And it's helpful to have a record of what whiskies you've tried, which ones you like (and don't like), and what you thought about them.

HOW DO I CHOOSE THE BEST BOTTLE OF WHISKY?

Honestly, most of the indicators for "better" whisky are myths. Older isn't always better. More expensive isn't always better. Darker colored isn't always better. No particular style (like single malt) is "better."

Personal preference is king. If you want delicate and fruity, find a Scottish or Japanese single malt boasting these qualities. If you want sweet vanilla and caramel, go with bourbon. If you want something powerful and primal, find a peated whisky serving up smoky, medicinal, or seaweed-y notes. If you want robust and spicy, find a high ABV rye.

If you're looking for flavor, avoid the cheapest whiskies. They're designed to be as approachable and popular as possible. It's not that they're bad. They're just . . . less. It's worth spending an extra 10 or 20 bucks for a bottle with more personality.

Higher ABV whiskies will often have greater character. More alcohol is an indicator that a whisky's not just aimed at the mass market. When a distiller bottles a whisky at a higher strength, they do it for flavor reasons.

If I'm buying a gift for a whisky nerd, I'll try to find something they haven't tried: a bottle from a small distillery, or a single barrel whisky, or a limited edition. If I'm buying a gift for someone who's not a whisky nerd, I'll play it safe with an all-rounder: approachable, flavorsome enough to drink on its own, balanced enough to mix. Maybe a nice Irish whiskey, or a Glenmorangie Original.

Instead of asking, "What's the best whisky?" ask, "What's the best whisky for *me*, or for *this situation?*" If I want something to grab from the cupboard whenever I feel like an easy drink, I'll get a bourbon that balances taste with bang for buck (Maker's Mark is a solid option). But if I'm having friends over for pre-dinner cocktails, I'll spend more for something interesting that'll excite the foodies.

I STRUGGLE TO PICK OUT TASTING NOTES IN WHISKY. WHAT'S WRONG WITH ME?

You probably have a rare tasting disease. Either that, or you're just a very stupid person.

Or maybe – just maybe – you're completely normal, and everyone finds this difficult until they've developed their whisky palate with a lot of practice.

We're not talking about a bag of Skittles here, where you pluck out one flavor at a time. We're talking about a complex spirit full of flavor compounds that have been infusing together for years to create a harmonious blend. Oh, and it's high enough in alcohol to burn your nostrils, tongue, and throat if you're not careful.

Of course it's hard to pick out individual flavor notes!

It's true that some people have natural ability – we all have a different sense of taste, so some people are more attuned to certain flavors than others.

But tasting is also a skill that can be improved with practice. If you want to do this in a focused way, flick back to "Tasting whisky" on page 109 for some tips.

You don't have to overthink it – just keep drinking different whiskies, be patient, and pay attention. Chase down a whisky flavor wheel if you want guidance in finding the right words. But if you never get past describing a whisky as "caramelly or fruity" that's absolutely fine.

Is the goal to become a whisky writer who rambles on about crème brûlée made with Madagascan vanilla beans and blackberries ripened under the full moon? (Fair warning: not a lucrative career path.)

Or is the goal to enjoy your whisky?

Because you can do that – even with your rare tasting disease.

CAN I MAKE MY OWN WHISKY?

Home distilling brings together the slight risk of accidental poisoning, the slightly higher risk of fires and explosions, and the certainty of making alcohol that isn't being taxed – and governments particularly hate that last one. So it's illegal to distill alcohol at home in most countries, at least without proper licensing.

But there are other ways you can play around with whisky creations.

The easiest is flavoring whisky – you can infuse it with fruits, nuts or spices (see "Making whisky and food work together – Infusions" on page 209), or try fat washing (see "Making cocktails – Fat washing" on page 149).

It's also perfectly legal to buy new make or moonshine and age it yourself. You can buy small oak barrels that hold a few liters, or you can go smaller again with bottle aging. Instead of putting spirit into a barrel, put the barrel into the spirit! That is, you can get pieces of charred oak staves designed for this, which can produce something that resembles whisky in a couple of months rather than years.

If you're determined to go the whole hog, and you're willing to get the right paperwork to do it properly, know that making good whisky is no simple task. Many of your favorite distilleries have spent hundreds of years honing their recipes, learning from their mistakes, and bringing together the best grain, local spring water, tried-and-tested yeast strains, and expertly selected casks they can get their hands on. Unsurprisingly, it's hard to make the same product in your garage with a copper kettle and a bag of wood chips.

But don't let my naysaying stop you! Find your nearest distilling store. Join a few online forums, where obsessed hobbyists share recipes and discuss technicalities like modern-day alchemists. You'll be a mad scientist in no time.

CAN I SEE HOW WHISKY IS MADE?

Yep! Most distilleries offer tours, and some even run whisky-blending workshops. Smell the mash and the spirit. Run your hand over the oak. Get a splinter.

At smaller distilleries, you can often talk with the owner or distiller. Take the chance to ask questions; if you ask nicely, they might even give you a peek behind the scenes.

You can also trawl the internet for videos and virtual tours of distilleries around the world. Lagavulin has an interactive 360-degree virtual tour – pour yourself a dram and experience it in your lounge room.

WILL WHISKY GO BAD? HOW DO I STORE IT? WILL IT KEEP AGING?

Whisky's tough. The high alcohol content protects it from nasties. A bottle that's been opened will see slight changes over time, but it's not a huge deal. Some people even prefer whisky after the flavors have "opened up" for a few months or years. But whisky's not invincible – while it won't spoil like milk, it can be affected by air, light, temperature, and evaporation.

An unopened bottle is pretty safe. You could bury it like pirate treasure, and it'll be fine when you dig it up.

Once a bottle of whisky's been opened, its flavors won't stay at their best forever. Almost full? Good for a few years. Less than half full? Consider it your mission to finish it within six to 12 months.

The best practice is to store it somewhere cool, dark, and dry, like your pantry. Stand it upright. Make sure the lid's on tight. Keep out of reach of sneaky babysitters.

But if you prefer to keep your collection on display in a drinks cabinet, go ahead. As long as it's not in direct sunlight or somewhere that gets hot, you shouldn't have a problem.

The only issue I've had with keeping whisky on display? It's always looking at me, teasing me, tempting me, calling me . . .

Will it continue to age? No. Wood is the magic ingredient, so once whisky is out of barrel and into bottle, the maturation is finished. A 10-year-old whisky is still a 10-year-old whisky, even if it's been in your pantry for years.

WHAT'S THE BEST WAY TO INTRODUCE MY FRIENDS TO WHISKY?

Chances are, some of your friends have had only limited – or bad – experiences of whisky. Rather than calling them to worship at The Altar Of Barley And Barrel, host a fun event to show your friends a different side of whisky. It's not your job to "convert" anyone, but giving people a chance to try whisky in interesting new ways can help throw off some of the myths and stereotypes.

Here's a few ideas:

Buy an interesting bottle and serve it up as a highball, as an old fashioned, and a whiskey sour. If your friends are new to whisky, they'll be surprised at how diverse it can be.

Serve up a few unidentified whiskies to your guests, as well as a mix of tasting notes or online reviews (minus any details that'd give away the whiskies' identities). As everyone tastes, they try to match each whisky to its respective description. Do you let them discuss and debate, or make them compete against each other? Do you slip in some fake tasting notes and reviews to make it harder? You can have a lot of fun with this!

Bourbon and BBQ. Rye and apple pie. Irish coffee and croissants. This can be as elaborate or as simple as you want, and people will still be impressed.

Your friends may have tried whisky with cola or ginger ale, but have they tried it with iced tea, coconut water, or freshly pressed apple juice?

HOW DO I MEET OTHER WHISKY LOVERS?

Whisky clubs and events are a great way to meet like-minded people – and to geek out without annoying your friends and family.

Most whisky bars run regular tastings and events. You can join an organization like the Scotch Malt Whisky Society, which has branches all over the world. And unless you live in the middle of nowhere, you should have no problem finding a whisky club.

I'm also a big fan of starting your own whisky club. It's a good excuse to catch up with your friends regularly and go on a whisky journey together, and a way to taste lots of different whiskies without having to sell a kidney.

Here are some ideas:

Taste three or four whiskies following a theme – all from the same region, or in the same style – to explore what's similar and what's different between them. Or choose whiskies based on their differences – each with a different base grain or finished in a different cask.

Take turns researching a topic to present to the group – a region, a distillery, an ingredient, a process, a style.

Order a tasting pack from a distillery or other online service.

Watch a virtual distillery tour or video of a guided tasting through a distillery's offerings.

Taste one whisky with different mixers, or as different cocktails.

Or just get together once a month to drink old fashioneds and listen to '80s rock. It still counts.

IS THERE NON-ALCOHOLIC WHISKY?

Yes . . . ish.

Whisky's high alcohol strength and years spent in oak are what make it what it is; it's no easy task trying to capture its complexity and intensity without them. But there are indeed distilled non-alcoholic spirits intended to mimic the taste and experience of different whisky styles. For the most part, they're designed to be mixed, or to use in cocktails.

Are they any good? That's up to each person. I'll admit, I've only tasted a few, but none of them hit the spot. They may have added *something* to a drink, but it wasn't enough to feel like a worthwhile substitute for me – especially since they're not cheap.

Though I've found you can make a decent whiskey sour mocktail using an infusion of Assam tea, vanilla extract, and maple syrup for a bourbon-esque vibe.

IS THERE GLUTEN-FREE WHISKY?

Almost all whisky is gluten free, even if it's not marked on the bottle.

While barley and most other grains used to make whisky contain gluten, the gluten proteins can't pass through the distillation process. So as a rule, no distilled spirit contains gluten.

Of course, a spirit could pick up gluten after this point, such as some flavored whiskies, or whiskies aged in beer barrels. And in a distillery, there's the possibility of cross-contamination.

I'm not a doctor, scientist, or coeliac, so do your own research before guzzling a bottle of GlenGluten Single Malt. But many experts – and anecdotally, many coeliacs – say whisky is safe for those who can't tolerate gluten.

CAN I BUY A BARREL OF WHISKY TO GIVE TO MY BABY WHEN THEY COME OF AGE?

You can . . . but honestly, I wouldn't recommend it.

Between shipping (possibly even importing), storage, and getting the whisky bottled . . . the costs and logistics are a nightmare.

Any single cask of whisky is an unknown, especially for an amateur. You don't know how it will age. Will it reach its prime in six years, or eight, or ten? By 18 or 21 years it could be over-oaked and over the hill.

Your child may not like whisky! Wouldn't that be a kick in the teeth?

And even if they do like it, they now have hundreds of bottles of the exact same whisky. Even most committed drinkers would find that more of a burden than a gift.

If you want my two cents: forget about buying a barrel. Wait until your child comes of age, then buy them a nice bottle. Sitting down with them, sharing a drink, teaching them how to enjoy whisky . . . that's a much better gift.

WHERE DO I GO FROM HERE?

Get to know other whisky drinkers. Go to your local whisky bar and make friends with other punters and with the staff. Go to events and masterclasses and whisky festivals. Join online communities and chat on forums. Send a message to your favorite whisky bloggers and Instagrammers.

Visit distilleries and see where whisky's made. Talk to the people who make and sell whisky – especially those who see it as a passion more than a product. Ask them how they recommend drinking their whisky.

Find whisky experiences. Go to tastings, distillery tours, and whisky-blending workshops. Check out the whisky scene when you travel overseas, or even plan a trip around visiting your favorite distilleries. And don't forget to hit up the duty-free shop on your way home!

The most important thing? Keep having fun with whisky. By all means, go down the rabbit hole, learn more about it – heck, even write a book about it – but you don't always have to take whisky seriously. And whatever you do, please don't become a whisky wanker. The world of whisky already has more than its fair share of snobs who tell people whisky must be drunk a certain way. It doesn't need another one.

Whisky was built on the backs of moonshiners, bootleggers, and revolutionaries. It can handle a bit of rule breaking. Drink what you enjoy, the way you enjoy it – even if it means ignoring everything in this book.

ACKNOWLEDGMENTS

So many people deserve credit for this book . . .

The team at Rockpool Publishing. Lisa and Paul run a good ship; I can't thank them enough for their patience and understanding when things didn't go to plan. I'm also grateful to all the Rockpool team members who worked to bring this book into the world.

Heather Millar, for editing my words. Thanks for polishing a rough rock into a gleaming gem.

Ellie Grant, for filling my books with funky illustrations. People are always saying how great your artwork is, and you deserve every single bit of praise.

Sam Slaney at Starward, who helped me get my head around the finer points of making whisky – especially the differences between old school and new school.

Luke McCarthy, who shared his insights into the questions people have, and the gaps he sees in whisky education.

David Rogalsky and Shane Fairweather at Noosa Heads Distillery, for letting me poke my nose into every nook and cranny of the distillery – and into their fine whisky!

My incredible wife Kamina. She researched, she edited, she sat with me late at night, and she held down the fort in our household when I was busy or distracted. She gave so much of herself to help get this book over the line. She's the best.

My little boy. Every day, he invited me to play and read with him. Every day, even in the stressful times, he made me smile and laugh and glow with love. Thanks buddy.

ABOUT THE AUTHOR

Mick Wüst is an award-winning booze writer who's been rambling about alcohol since 2015. When he's not drinking whisky and writing books, he's drinking coffee and reading trashy action novels. He's worked as a pastor, a lecturer and a barista, and is still working toward his dream job as a Professional Sandwich Eater. He lives in Brisbane (the best city) with his wife and son (the best people).

This is Mick's third book, following *Beer Drinker's Toolkit* and *Gin Drinker's Toolkit.* He's expecting a call from George Lucas or Steven Spielberg to discuss film rights for the trilogy.

You can find Mick on Facebook and Instagram as Schoonerversity.

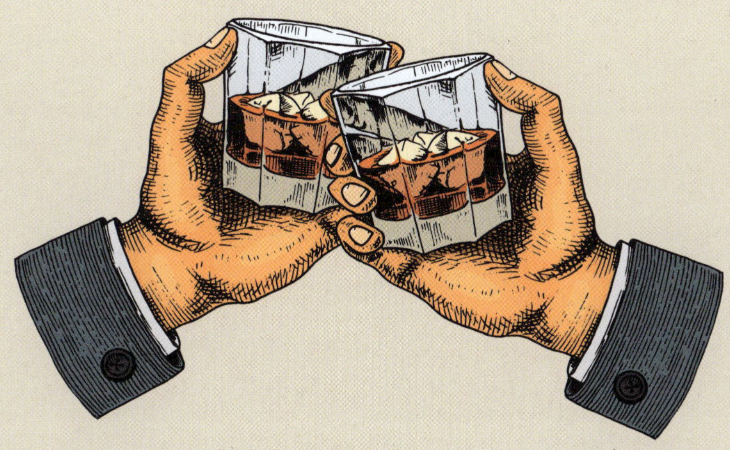